M000217911

"Lindi Tardif tells an awesome story of breaking the mental chains of racist apartheid and building a life of freedom and meaning. 'Inspirational' is an overused word, but in this case it's the best way to describe her book."
—**Benjamin Pogrund**
Recipient of the National Order of Ikhamanga in Silver; author of books about Robert Mangaliso Sobukwe, Nelson Mandela, the Press under apartheid, and Israel and apartheid; and former Deputy Editor, Rand Daily Mail, Johannesburg.

"Lindi's account of the evils of racism is moving and her comments on the way forward are compelling though I would implore us to keep in mind that we were created by God as one human race and that seeing ourselves as separate races keeps us trapped in the deception of racism."
—**Evangelist Alveda King**
American activist; author of several books including *King Truths: 21 Keys To Unlocking Your Spiritual Potential, America Return To God*; and Executive Director, Civil Rights for the Unborn with Priests for Life.

"Without grasping for hyperbole or sensationalism, Lindi Tardif has written about some of the most difficult circumstances of life in the most human of terms. She takes the reader through situations that would leave most people hardened, hateful, and bitter and then shows us that there is another way. It is the way of forgiveness and ultimately, the way of love. Love of life, love of family, love of her fellow people, and love of God. This book is the illumination of a path that is too frequently left unnoticed in the shadows and passed by. Lindi has a lot to say, and it is worth the time to read it, and then some."
—**Dale Font**
Conservative Leader, Woodinville, Washington State.

"Beyond a beautifully moving and deeply engaging account of family and identity and of race and reconciliation, in *Daughter of Apartheid*, Lindi adroitly navigates the ups and downs of her life as a woman of color, and deftly weaves richly-hued vignettes of some of her compatriots in and out the primary narrative. Tracing her extraordinary journey from the dusty, apartheid-era townships of segregated South Africa to the shiny spires of corporate America, the book also provides a reflective 'must read' at critical milieus in both these nations' histories, serving as a thoughtful bridge between White and Black readers and those of every shade in between, and charting a profoundly practical course for both decision-makers and their diverse constituents alike toward the more perfect union that we are all beholden to. Her richly rewarding narrative ultimately serves as a call to action, challenging the reader to think more deeply and emboldening us to act courageously, moving us beyond fear and toward hope."

—Sebastian Matthews
Board Director, Global Evergreen Alliance

DAUGHTER OF APARTHEID

DAUGHTER OF APARTHEID

Lindi Tardif

ELM HILL

A Division of
HarperCollins Christian Publishing

www.elmhillbooks.com

Daughter of Apartheid

Published in Nashville, Tennessee, by Elm Hill, an imprint of Thomas Nelson. Elm Hill and Thomas Nelson are registered trademarks of HarperCollins Christian Publishing, Inc.

Elm Hill titles may be purchased in bulk for educational, business, fund-raising, or sales promotional use. For information, please e-mail SpecialMarkets@ ThomasNelson.com.

The author has tried to recreate events, locations, and conversations from her memories of them. The conversations are not written in a way that represents word-for-word transcripts. The author has instead retold them in a way that evokes the feeling and meaning of what was said and in all instances, the essence of the dialogue is accurate. Although the author has made every effort to ensure that the information in this book was correct at press time, the author does not assume and hereby disclaims any liability to any party for any loss, damage, or disruption caused by errors or omissions, whether such errors or omissions result from negligence, accident, or any other cause. The opinions expressed by the author represent her personal views and should not be ascribed to her employer; any individuals, corporations, and institutions named in this book; and any other person. The narrative of her friends, family members, and teachers should also not be ascribed to third parties.

Library of Congress Cataloging-in-Publication Data

Library of Congress Control Number: 2019933673

ISBN 978-1-400325269 (Paperback)
ISBN 978-1-400325276 (Hardbound)
ISBN 978-1-400325283 (eBook)

DEDICATION

*To Amelia, Naledi, and Abraham: learn from my mistakes,
and whatever happens, please don't drop the baton.
Keep the light shining!*

*To my English teacher, the late Solly Ismail, who helped reinforce a
key lesson my mom tried to teach me, and to Herschel Alpert
and Michelle Garcia, my mentors and supporters in
the profession, thank you. You guys rock!*

TABLE OF CONTENTS

FOREWORD

In recent times there has been a sharp increase in published works by young South Africans, telling the stories of their lives under or after apartheid. The biographies of post-apartheid youth often tell the stories that came after with bitterness and stridency, such as Malaika Wa Azania's *Memoirs of a Born Free* or Rekgotsofetse Chikane's *Breaking a Rainbow, Building a Nation*. These are important books, for they give insight into the anger and anxieties of young South Africans born after Nelson Mandela's release from prison, who were children during the early years of democracy. Such works, moreover, allow us to measure the pulse of one segment of South African youth, on the cusp of becoming national leaders in politics and the professions.

There is, however, one major limitation with angry writing—it is sharp on analysis but offers few options for a radically different society that recognizes the inherent value of all South Africans and the strategic importance of solidarity in dismantling the legacies of colonialism and apartheid. This is what is so different about Lindi Tardif's remarkable (though far too short) book, *Daughter of Apartheid*. Modestly titled, this important contribution to after-apartheid memoirs is exceptional in part because of its restraint in telling a personal story that is inevitably political, and in part because of the felt authority of the author's writing in sharing her life in narrative form.

Lindi's life straddles two worlds. She lived under and after apartheid, and can therefore give an account of both disenfranchisement and democracy. She grew up in a Black township but attended one of the more progressive "open schools" of the apartheid era, Sacred Heart College in Observatory, Johannesburg. She lived in Soweto, the center of youth struggles in the 1970s, but now resides near the liberal city of Seattle, Washington, on the northwest coast of the United States of America. She was nurtured by a proud Black struggle family in Soweto, but married a White American partner. She became a South African citizen by birth but a patriotic American citizen by choice.

There is something powerful that such a richly cosmopolitan life allows one to see, though only if you wish to see it. Encountering White South Africans in the struggle who made life-threatening sacrifices gives her a different perspective on the simplistic narrative of "evil Whites" and "good Blacks." Learning schoolwork alongside White students, often from more liberal parents, enables a powerful social learning as well. The mere possibility of shared values creates grounds for solidarity even when Whites and Blacks come into the South African reality from vastly different experiences. Working in the U.S. at one of the world's best-known brands, Amazon, extends the horizons of one's thinking beyond the parochialism.

Of course the author was angry as she considered the toll of living under apartheid, and seeing older members of her family resist and as she thought about the injustices she suffered. The daily grind of humiliation dished out by the apartheid state existed alongside the constant threat of assault by gangsters from the same community preying on vulnerable women; her harrowing account of a potential "jackrolling" (the hijacking and repeated rape of a woman) incident in Soweto is unforgettable. There is every reason for outrage, for the very phenomenon of "jackrollers" is a byproduct of colonialism and apartheid's emasculation of Black men over the centuries.

But Lindi recognized the self-destructive power of anger and the self-imprisonment brought on oneself by an unforgiving heart. And so she dared to move from a state of capture — of self capture — into one of personal liberation that allowed her to act on the world in solidarity with those who shared common ground. The transition from anger to freedom can be long and difficult, but Lindi accomplished it with persistence. In this regard the author has one major advantage, and that is her commitment to reason and the willingness to stand up to a crowd. As with the threatening "jackrolling" encounter, she stood up as a student leader to male activists at the University of the Witwatersrand, whose only sense of radical action was the violent disruption of the education of others. Lindi stood her ground and made the case for other radical options that could transform her university. It is such capacity for independence and reason that is sorely lacking in campus cultures in South Africa in the wake of the historic university student protests of 2015–2016.

It is seldom the case that a new author writes with such fluency and insight on a complex and devastating phenomenon like apartheid. As this short book drew to a close, I wanted to read more and learn more; for even as one who also straddles the worlds before and after apartheid, I find that Lindi brings to light new learnings, among which the most important must be that there are grounds for hope in the aftermath of South Africa's cataclysmic past. This is, therefore, a book that must be read in societies such as the USA and South Africa, where a very "present past" haunts our lives still.

Jonathan D. Jansen
Distinguished Professor of Education
University of Stellenbosch
South Africa

Introduction

I am a daughter of apartheid, born to an unapologetically racist system of economic slavery designed by and for a minority who considered the majority to be "less than" in every way. The system was called apartheid, an Afrikaans word meaning "separateness." But this was not separateness based on trivial differences such as "We cheer for baseball while you prefer cricket," or even more substantial differences like "We are Catholic, and you are Jewish." No, this separateness sprang from the belief that God had gifted the southern slice of Africa to a tiny group of people who had come from distant Holland and who had no connection to this land other than this one belief.

Strengthened by the influx of other Europeans, by the early twentieth century they had established economic, legal, cultural, and linguistic dominance over the country. In the middle of that century, in 1948, this minority formalized their control under the umbrella of apartheid. Not full-fledged slavery, yet far from freedom, it beggared eighty percent of the people, eventually restricting the bulk of the majority—those classified as Black[1]—to "homelands," artificially created "independent nations" within South Africa that were bereft of natural resources and unable to support the large number of people suddenly forced to scratch their soils in hope of survival. These tens of millions had no choice but to hold hats in hand and hope to be allowed to work in South Africa "proper." But when granted permission to enter South Africa, they were forced to inhabit an almost completely separate sphere, coming into contact with the ruling minority almost solely when working for them in menial positions.

Others in the oppressed majority—those classified as Indian and Coloured[2]—were similarly kept separate from the ruling minority, although their restrictions were a little less severe. Allowed to open small shops, serve in a restricted number of trades and even some professions, the Indians and Coloureds were legally separated not only from the ruling minority but also from each other as well as from the Blacks. For, you see, the ruling minority didn't feel it was sufficient to separate themselves from all others. It also forcibly split the majority into three distinct groups—Indian, Coloured, and Black—before further dividing Blacks by trying to drive wedges between the various tribes and even physically separating them geographically according to tribe. This was done in order to create a secondary system of separateness that made it more difficult for the "others" to coalesce as one, a separateness that bred resentment among the groups.

Apartheid was not an entirely new concept, for it echoed elements of the American system of "Jim Crow" and the country's reservation-based treatment of the Native Americans, the caste system of India, Australia's treatment of the Aborigines, and laws and customs restricting the "lesser thans" in many other societies. And like so many other oppressive systems, apartheid clung tenaciously to life, turning, so to speak, to tanks and torture in an effort to remain in force. Only after years of bloodshed and international pressure did apartheid crumble, unleashing equal measures of joy and rage, hope and fear.

A child of this bigotry based on skin color, I understand what it is like to feel the pressure to internalize the feeling of being inferior; to know that your horizons are harshly limited by law, custom, and attitude; and even to realize, at an early age, that if you are horribly injured and there is no ambulance available designated for your race, all the other ambulances will sit idle rather than come to your aid. Yet I also know what it is like to be raised by loving parents and grandparents, to be encouraged by teachers and pastors, and even to be assisted by some of the very Whites whose race was oppressing mine. I know what it is like to nurture hope for a better future, even as the world around you grows increasingly violent and dangerous, and many of those around you sink into despair.

I call myself a daughter of apartheid not just because I was born and raised under that oppressive system, but also because I was among the first wave of "oppressed others" to move into spheres of commerce that until very recently had been beyond our reach. This was even more the case for me because not only am I Black, I was a young woman in what was still very much a White, male-dominated workplace. Some of my bosses and colleagues viewed me with curiosity, some with disdain; to some I was a threat, while to others I was simply something to tolerate. Stepping onto the bottom rungs of large, formerly predominately White legal and public accounting firms was all so new, so different than anything I had ever known. And so often, it was incredibly frustrating because for the first time, I fully experienced what it's like to be treated as something "different" and apart from the predominant group.

While my childhood was difficult and sometimes outright dangerous, living as I did in ghetto-like conditions in the areas reserved for the "lessers," my young adulthood was confusing and filled with hurdles. Yet those years were fueled by hope, driven by choices I had made years before, and other choices that had been made on my behalf. I had a sense that for the first time in countless generations, I and those like me had the freedom to choose our own paths and maybe, just maybe, to succeed.

I was among those who came of age during a time of tremendous change; I straddled the divide between apartheid South Africa and the Rainbow Nation. Twenty years old when South Africa's first democratic elections took place in 1994, I literally lived almost half of my life under apartheid. Those who came before me knew only separation and oppression, while those who followed were born into the idea that, in the words of the constitution, "South Africa belongs to all who live in it, united in our diversity." My generation—perhaps it's not really a generation, but rather a seven- to ten-year cohort—knows both. Therefore, my generation has a unique perspective on what happened then as well as what is happening now—on transitioning from restriction to freedom; on recognizing and celebrating progress; on pushing through negatives to embrace forgiveness, hope, and humanity; and on understanding the importance of choice.

Twenty-some years past South Africa's rebirth, I am well into my career as a corporate international tax planning professional. I have traveled to many countries and been part of vastly different societies. I have enjoyed the delight of people predominantly responding to me on the basis of who I am rather than by my skin color. I married and gave birth to children across racial lines. I have seen that love knows no color and that color need not be a barrier to people connecting with each other at all levels. I have learned that past hurts and anger can be overcome, and I have seen people at their best. I have also seen societies and people far from this ideal.

In this mix of good and bad, I have seen that choice matters. I have learned that one always has choices, even if they are limited by circumstances. I have learned that life is driven by the choices made by individuals, families, small groups, large groups, entire societies, and nations.

We can always choose to view others on the basis of their humanity rather than by their skin color or the actions of their group. We can choose to reach out rather than close ourselves in. We can choose to study and to strive, even if our schools are subpar. We can decide, very deliberately, when we need to fight for our rights and how to do so in the most effective manner, in ways that, as far as possible, build bridges rather than tear them down. And we can also choose to release our anger, no matter how long and tenaciously we have clung to it, so that we may move forward.

Two decades past the fall of apartheid, a quarter century since the liberation of Eastern European states, five decades since the death of American "Jim Crow," seventy-plus years since the beginning of the emancipation of the African states, some Black people are still disappointed, angry, or embittered. In the United States, Black anger has coalesced around the Black Lives Matter movement, which posits that the state and "vigilantes" place a lower value on Black lives than on those of other groups, and that Black lives are "systematically targeted for demise." In South Africa, some Black people are angry that more than twenty years post-apartheid they still do not have access to the country's resources.

I wrote this book in hope that it will speak to all who feel embittered or that they are not receiving their full measure of rights and opportunities and that "the system" is still rigged against them.

In essence, this is my message: I was born into a racist system designed to make me and those like me into "economic slaves" whose mere presence soiled the atmosphere and could only be tolerated in small doses. I was born and raised in what was, at that time, an impoverished and often dangerous Black residential area. I might have spent my life poor and uneducated, angry and bitter, feeling victimized in every way by "the man." Instead, I chose to embrace faith, hard work, forgiveness, and openness to others, and to avail myself of all the resources at my disposal, meager though they were. I don't claim to be superior in any way, for I realize that in my youth, I was guided to many of these choices by my faith, parents, teachers, pastors, and others. Had circumstances been different, I might have made different choices. Nevertheless, these were my choices, and as I grew older and exercised more control over my life, they became more and more "mine." And as I grew older, I saw how the choices made by others led them down paths that became increasingly restricted, embittering, separated from others, and cut off from opportunities. I am thankful that I was guided toward affirming choices.

Through this book I tell my story—and the stories of some of my friends and teachers—in the hope that these stories may be helpful to those wrestling with the challenges of our times. My personal story will be presented in bits and pieces out of chronological order, for this is not an autobiography. Instead, the various story segments will be used to illustrate the issues I have grappled with, including issues of choice, identity, forgiveness, and humanity.

I chose this approach because I believe in the African tradition and power of storytelling, in the new understandings that often emerge when people listen to one another and listen solely to hear, not to judge or critique. Listening in this way is a gesture of humanity—what Africans refer to as the spirit of *ubuntu*[3]—for when you listen with open ears and an open heart, you cannot help but learn something, be touched, or in some other manner step away from your prejudgments, if only a little. And with each of those little steps we take, we all move closer to healing and reconciliation.

CHAPTER ONE

OUR CHOICES MATTER

I grew up in Soweto—that's what everyone called the South Western Townships—an enormous, disjointed series of townships just outside of Johannesburg to the south. Imagine thousands and thousands of tiny houses—some no more than shacks, really—jammed one against the other with jerry-rigged electrical and power supplies. Imagine streets often paved with dirt and some now and then coated with waste that oozed up from broken sewer pipes. No malls, no parks, no beauty parlors, no coffee shops, and no friendly cops on the beat to protect you—for protecting us was the lowest priority, and residents knew better than to even call for help. This was the Soweto I knew as a girl and a teen in the 1980s. There were certainly nicer areas of Soweto such as Dube and Diepkloof Extension, but remember, I'm using the word "nicer" in the context of apartheid.

In 1976, two years after I was born, Soweto began to bleed, literally. Outraged when the government decreed that Black students would now be taught in Afrikaans—the language of apartheid—rather than in Zulu, Sotho, or one of the other indigenous tongues, students rallied in the streets. As many as twenty thousand left their classrooms to march, and this time, the police rushed to our "aid" armed with dogs, automatic rifles, and armored cars. No one knows exactly how many people were killed, but the estimates range up to seven hundred.

Things settled down a bit after the initial wave of protests, and through the rest of my first ten years, life was fairly calm. For the most part, I lived on Khuzwayo Street in Orlando East with my maternal grandparents Irene Deliwe and John Hosea Langa, plus Trevor, their adopted son. I lived there because it was within walking distance of a private Catholic school called St. John Berchman's that my family wanted me to attend. The four of us shared a three-room house consisting of a bedroom, kitchen, and living room, and we washed up in basins, which required boiling water every morning to prepare for work or school.

A little room containing nothing but the toilet sat in the back yard, a ways back from the house. There was no lighting outside the house except a single naked bulb that at best threw a few weak rays in the direction of the outhouse. We were not among the fortunate few who had a streetlight near their house, and a flashlight was an unimaginable luxury, so a night-time trip through the deeply shadowed back yard to the outhouse was always a bit frightening. We kept a bucket in the house that we used to relieve ourselves during the night.

For much of my childhood, I had no concept of life outside of Soweto. For me, it was perfectly natural to see families with two parents, some children, a grandparent, and a distant relative or two sharing a three-room house. As far as I knew, every community had trash on the roads and in piles on the sidewalks. It seemed normal for young men to be hanging around in little gangs on the streets and for girls to drop out of school because they became pregnant.

I hadn't realized how ghetto-like Soweto was until I began attending the Dominican Convent School in Belgravia (known as "Belgravia Convent" then) in 1985, and later, a high school called Sacred Heart College (known as "Sacred Heart") in Observatory. Both of these were mixed-race, private Catholic schools, among the relatively few schools to flout apartheid by allowing racial groups to mix and offering a good education to all.

Observatory was a lovely middle-class, White suburb where all the streets were clean and paved, the houses were large and neatly lined up along the streets, and inside, they were so spacious they could have held three or four of my house. And they had massive yards, some with swimming pools and tennis courts. Seeing these things and realizing how "wealthy" almost all Whites were compared to almost all Blacks made me realize that Soweto wasn't a place that just happened to be poor. It was what it was because of apartheid, and I hated that.

Another thing I noticed was how safe these White neighborhoods were. Earlier, I mentioned there had been protests over the awful state of Black education when I was a toddler. Things had quieted down until around my tenth birthday, when school boycotts began again in earnest, and the level of violence seemed to shoot up. Not only was there violence directed at the government, but the community itself was awash in crime, petty and violent, for it had become home to numerous *tsotsis*[4] who knew they had nothing to fear from the absent police. The community learned to treat the *tsotsis* with respect, as failing to do so would anger them. It learned to turn the other way when these criminals went on a rampage and to pretend afterward that nothing had happened, rather than risk a confrontation that could go terribly wrong.

Every school day, I put on my school uniform and made the trip from Soweto to the nice White neighborhood, returning home in the afternoon. Looking back, I realize this was not the best idea. I should have worn my school clothes only at school, for wearing them in the streets of Soweto drew a lot of attention, and attention drawn by a young woman was, by definition, dangerous. One day when I was about sixteen years old, I was returning home from Sacred Heart. The taxi dropped me off on Tema Street, and from there, I walked the third of a mile to my grandmother's house. A car suddenly appeared alongside me, its windows rolled down and three guys inside. The car was ordinary—a light-brown, four-door sedan—as were the guys, who appeared to be around eighteen or twenty years old. I can't tell you much more than that because I was trying very hard to keep looking ahead. I knew that giving them more than a quick glance would be interpreted as an invitation to continue.

"Get inside," one of them said to me in Zulu. His voice was sort of friendly, but this was a command, not a request. I walked on, not responding. He kept repeating the command as the car rolled along beside me, matching my pace. I just kept walking and looking straight ahead, engaging with them as little as possible. I'd been propositioned by neighborhood boys before, even by *tsotsis*, but they left me alone once they realized I was not interested and would not accede to their demands. The show-no-interest-and-dig-your-heels-in strategy usually worked, but this time it failed. The car kept rolling along beside me, with the guy growing more and more insistent.

Then it dawned on me: this was more than a proposition. *Oh, my God!* I thought. *I'm being jackrolled!*

Jackrolling might seem like a quaint expression—cute, almost—but it was the worst thing that could happen to a woman. To be jackrolled meant to be snatched off the street by a group of guys, stuffed into their car, driven off somewhere, and raped repeatedly, at least once by each of the guys, maybe more. Most women who were jackrolled did not live to tell the tale.

I knew that once you were in the car, you were finished, so I kept walking, staring, and strolling ahead as if nothing were wrong, for to show any sign of weakness would spur them on. "Come on, cutie, get in," one of them ordered in Zulu again. I could hear the others saying something to each other but couldn't make it out. I kept walking.

I had repeatedly refused to obey, and now they were angry. They continued driving slowly alongside me, their voices increasingly insistent, their tone growing louder, and their words harsher.

People saw what was happening and started gathering in a group near the corner of Tema and Mzinyane Streets. In what seemed like a few seconds, there were about twenty people standing in front of the house, watching. Just watching. No one said anything, no one challenged the guys, no one motioned for me to hurry into their house. That wasn't how things were done, even though many of these people recognized me, and some even knew my family. You just didn't get involved; it was too dangerous. If you intervened, the jackrollers would come after you right there and then, and the police wouldn't protect you, as they were generally absent. (You couldn't just summon them with a 911 call.) Nobody dared do more than stand there. The neighborhood watched this drama unfold as quietly and passively as if they were watching an episode of a crime show on TV.

And me? I just kept walking, looking ahead, letting my body language signal "no" over and over again, not getting in the car, and not allowing my body to betray any anger, any fear, any anything. I knew the worst thing I could do was to show fear or to cry, for both would be seen as signs of weakness.

Then one of them hopped out of the car. He was thin, of medium height, with short hair. Nothing about his appearance was memorable except the menace in his eyes. I knew he was going to grab me. I stopped dead in my tracks, knowing that I had to stand my ground. Doing so probably wouldn't help, but to back down, cry, or run would certainly lead to disaster.

I was terrified. There was no way I could get away from these three guys, and no one was going to come to my aid. There was nothing to do but ask for help. *Oh God!* my heart cried out. *You have to help me! I'm not going to convince these guys to let me go, and no one is helping me.*

I just stood there, hoping something would happen. Then suddenly, one of the guys in the back of the car said, *"Yazini? Yekani les' sfebe!"*—meaning, "You know what? Leave this whore alone."

"Ja," said the driver, *"yeka les' sfebe."*

Without a word, the guy I feared would grab me sauntered back to the car and got in, and they drove off.

And that was that; it was all over. People returned to their homes as quietly as they had come out. No one asked me if I was all right, no one gave me a reassuring smile, and no one nodded a greeting. It was just another day, another almost-jackrolling, another incident that filled the neighborhood with fear and anger that no one would acknowledge, for living with intimidation was so very routine.

It's All about Choice

I haven't thought about this much over the years because it was, indeed, so routine. And now I realize that it *had* to remain routine in my mind; otherwise, I might have broken down in tears. There wasn't anything I could do about jackrolling, life in Soweto, or apartheid—except to make the choices I believed would help me make a better life for myself someday, somehow. I had to choose to avoid compromising situations with boys that could lead to my becoming a parent before I was ready, choose to steer clear of friends who were bad influences, choose to get the best education available to Blacks, and above all, choose to hold on to my faith and remain strong.

That was my only power: choice.

Even though we as a people hardly had any power of choice, the idea that I had choice and the responsibility to exercise it wisely was ingrained in me from an early age. My mother, Esther Happy Langa, never told me I couldn't drink, smoke, do drugs, neglect my homework, hang out with boys, or anything else. Instead she said, "Lindi, you have the freedom to do whatever you want, make any choice you like. But remember: you are not free from the consequences of that choice." She was teaching me an important lesson, which was that life doesn't "just happen." Instead it is driven by the many choices we make. Yes, there are limitations created by choices other people have made, often before we are born. Apartheid slapped severe limitations on the lives of all of the "others," and there were additional restrictions imposed by family, economic circumstances, geography, and other factors. But no matter how bound our lives may be, there are *always* choices to make, and we are *always* affected by the results of those choices.

When the jackrollers pulled up beside me, I chose not to break down and cry, and I chose not to comply. I made the choice to risk infuriating them by demanding my dignity and saying no. Things might have gone much worse for me because of this, and other women may have gotten into the car in hopes of keeping the damage level low, relatively speaking, or maybe even talking the jackrollers out of it. Those were common strategies, and it's not for me to judge others. When you're in that situation, your fear level leaps off the charts, and you grasp at any straw that pops into your terrified mind. I can only say that for me, the choice was clear: even if they beat me fiercely because of it, my answer was no. I felt that if I didn't stand my ground, I would be raped multiple times, possibly impregnated, or killed—so my answer was no. I was not getting in that car! That was my choice, and I was willing to accept the consequences of making it.

CHAPTER TWO

LANGA WOMEN DON'T CRY

I lived in my grandparents' home in Orlando East between the ages of four and ten, and again from thirteen to seventeen. When I returned at age thirteen, Grandfather had already passed away, and Trevor was unfortunately spending many nights away. So it was usually just me and my grandmother, whom I called Mamkhulu—a Zulu word meaning "big momma"—instead of the more common "Gogo," which means granny. In truth, Mamkhulu wasn't big physically. She was only about five feet, five inches tall, but she loomed large in my life. My grandfather John had devoted much of his time to protecting the Black community from the authorities; I guess he is best described as a "community activist." Unfortunately, you're not paid for being a community activist in a community where almost everyone lives either on the edge of poverty or in it. This means that it was up to Mamkhulu to be the family breadwinner while raising my mom and later spending a lot of time caring for me and Trevor. Grandfather died when Mamkhulu was fifty years old—or maybe older, not even she is quite sure—leaving behind no money, no property, no stocks or bonds, and no valuable coins or rare stamps hidden in a little box in the rafters. He did leave behind an opportunity, which I'll talk about in a later chapter. But you can't buy food or pay utility bills with that, so Mamkhulu continued rising at five in the morning to begin her long days.

Mamkhulu had originally qualified as a nurse but her job required her to work at night, and traveling between work and home while it was dark was not the safest thing to do. Grandfather insisted she get a "regular" job, and so she did, working as a cashier in a furniture shop in Johannesburg. She handled sales as well as monthly layaway payments, which she carefully tracked in her ledger. The fact that she was well-educated meant she was qualified to rise up and perhaps become a manager or even a department head, but that's not how things were back then—not for Blacks.

Not only was advancement out of the question, but her job itself always hung in the balance. You see, there were a lot of Blacks competing for the relatively small number of "good" jobs open to them, like being a cashier in a store or bank. Rarely would you be promoted or even transferred to other positions on the same level as your job because these jobs were mostly reserved for Whites, so you had no choice but to cling desperately to what you had. You were as good a worker as you possibly could be, rarely asking for any time off to handle a personal or family emergency, and never, ever showing signs of resentment or talking back. As a Black person, you understood that the people you were working for had been conditioned to believe that you were by nature a lazy, larcenous liar. The "better Blacks," according to apartheid conditioning, could be relied upon, more or less. But the slightest misstep—which included asking for a day off because you were sick—might mean being dismissed. Yes, there were some employers, including White ones, who valued you as a person and cared about you. But for the most part, a Black employee was just another cog in the wheel to be replaced as soon as it showed any sign of wear. Plenty of other Blacks were eager to be your replacement, not because they liked the situation any more than you did, but because they had families to feed.

"You had fear of the White man," Mamkhulu said over and over when I spoke to her in preparation for writing this book. "If they said, 'Be there at seven in the morning,' you were there at seven; if the rule was you had a thirty-minute break, that's what you took. You did what they said because you had fear of the White man." All it would have taken was a negative word or two uttered by a White person to jeopardize her livelihood.

Mamkhulu was an exemplary worker. Her books always balanced to the penny, and she was often sent to other branches to figure out where their clerks' accounts went awry. Despite this honor, she was never promoted and never rewarded with extra pay. To put it bluntly, the system stripped us Blacks of opportunities and of our humanity. Mamkhulu's generation knew that they were faceless and replaceable, and that their only recourse was to be strong enough to endure. This was Mamkhulu's response to apartheid: *Don't cry; don't feel sorry for yourself. Comply, hoping you'll be left alone. Do what it takes to survive.* Given that her husband did not have an income and the responsibility of feeding the family rested on her shoulders, being an exemplary employee was a reasonable choice.

Your Chore Is to Study

I didn't understand this when I was young, of course. I simply knew that Mamkhulu and I rose every morning at five, while it was still dark and cold. There was a coal stove we could have lit, but it would have been a waste of coal to warm the house for the sixty or so minutes before we left for work and school, and it required quite an effort to light it up. So for many months of the year, we simply endured the cold.

Our daily routine began with Mamkhulu boiling water on the stove and pouring it into a little orange basin we kept in the kitchen. This was her "morning bath." She would dip a cloth in the water, rub some soap on the cloth, and then wash herself from her head down, dipping the cloth back in the water and adding more soap every so often. When she was finished, she would discard the water and clean and refill the basin for me. While she was bathing, I would empty the bucket we kept under a chair in the bedroom—the one we used to pee in at night.

When school was in session, we were out of the house by six thirty and walking down the Orlando East streets, not all of which were paved, so they were muddy when it rained and dusty when the wind blew. The trip to school was lengthy once I left St. John Berchman's and began attending mixed-race private schools in distant so-called "White areas." When I was studying at Sacred Heart, the most economical means of transport was to walk about thirty minutes to the station and take a train to the place where I could catch the Sacred Heart school bus. From there, Mamkhulu would take a train to her job. Unfortunately, all this walking was hard on her, so we only did it for a few months. After that, we switched to walking five minutes to a local taxi (cab) rank and taking a taxi to Johannesburg's central business district. There, we would separate. She walked to her place of employment, and I took a bus to Sacred Heart. I didn't take the school bus but a public one clearly marked for "Whites, Indians, and Coloureds only," which meant I was breaking the law by using it, and so was the bus driver for allowing me to do so.

Mamkhulu was in her fifties during the years we did this, walking long distances from the house to work and back home at night. She left earlier than she had to in order to ensure that I got to school on time, and once she came home, she wouldn't let me do any chores. This was very unusual in the Black community, where it was expected that children would do a lot of household chores, and I mean a lot! But Mamkhulu wouldn't let me do any. "Your chore is to study," she would say. "You study, and I'll do this." And she did so, without fail, just as she marched to work every day for decades, stood on her feet for much of the day, and then marched home at night to her household chores, never missing a single day. It seemed as if this woman was made of iron, doing whatever was necessary to make sure I got a good education and had the teensy-tiniest chance of getting ahead.

This is not surprising, considering that her mother, whom I called Khokho, had instilled in Mamkhulu the value of education and of being vocally self-critical. (Khokho is a Swati/Zulu word meaning "great grandmother." Her given name was Gertrude Zodwa Dladla.)

Khokho, my great-grandmother, had been orphaned when she and her sister were young. They were taken in by relatives, and although their guardians were kind, they had no interest in educating the two young girls. For one thing, there was very little money to devote to schooling, and what they had, they used to buy books and other items for their own children. In addition, there was a feeling back then that there was no point in educating girls, for they would either become pregnant and drop out of school or marry and join their husband's family. Educating a son was a much better "investment" in the future. So Khokho was given only a basic education, then sent on to work as a maid. Fortunately, she wound up working for a wealthy Jewish family that took kindly to her and showed her special favor, which, in the context of apartheid, meant giving her cast-off clothing and furniture.

Khokho worked for this family for many years and was often struck by the fact that they were so orderly, well-groomed, and well-read. She decided that she wanted her children to be similarly well-bred, organized, and studious. As she traveled by train to and from work every day, she noticed that passengers on the "White" section of the train tended to read books or newspapers while commuting, while those in the "Black" section of the train tended not to. This reinforced the idea that her two children must learn how to read—not just learn, but excel. So she pushed her daughters, born 19 years apart, to make the best of themselves. Mamkhulu did so, excelling in math and science at school and later at nursing school. She performed so well there that the nursing school named an entire block of classrooms after her. Her younger sister, Duduzile Dladla, developed an interest in computers.

Since Khokho was often gone for much of the day working, young Mamkhulu was required to clean the entire house every morning before heading out to school and to cook dinner every day after returning home. How Mamkhulu managed to excel at her studies given these demands on her time is beyond my comprehension, but she did! And she did so dutifully, without crumbling under the pressure.

Years later, when I began school, my great-grandmother would tell me, "You need to learn and to read. It's important." Given Khokho's attitude toward reading and learning, it's no wonder that her daughter Mamkhulu wanted her own daughter (my mom Esther) and granddaughter to be educated. And for her, education included lessons in being strong, as she had been.

My Mother Hardly Ever Cried

The lesson on remaining strong was often reinforced in the discipline arena. When my mother was young, if she began crying while being disciplined, Mamkhulu would say to her, "You are not crying for a good reason. If you want a good reason to cry, I will give you a hiding." Mamkhulu was not cruel; she was simply teaching her daughter that there's no point in crying unless there's a really good reason to do so, and there is almost never a good enough reason.

"It got me to a place where I never cried," my mother said. "If my mother punished me for something I did, I wouldn't cry. We had corporal punishment in school. They would whip you for many reasons. I wouldn't cry when I was whipped; I would not give anyone the satisfaction of knowing they were hurting me. I took this attitude to work. As a Black person, you were in a system where the Whites were allowed to be cruel and ugly to you, and many were. When that happened, I wouldn't break down and feel sorry for myself. Other people would moan and cry; I never did. Even if a boss' criticism was unfair, I didn't cry. Instead, I thought about what I could do to eliminate this unfair criticism in the future. I was always thinking that I would never give anyone the satisfaction of seeing me hurting."

While Mamkhulu taught Mom to be strong, Grandfather taught my mother to demand her dignity, a very daring thing for a Black person to do back then, especially a Black woman. When Mom was in twelfth grade, she got a job with a home and garden store called Jacoby's. It was a clerical job, requiring her to walk up and down the store aisles, checking the merchandise, doing inventory, and arranging for more items to be brought to the shelves as requested. There were a number of other students her age performing the same job, each assigned to a certain set of aisles. Other than Mom and one other Black woman, they were all White.

"There was an old-school Afrikaans mentality at the store," Mom explained. "It was a somewhat hostile environment. Not completely unfriendly, because the other Black person and I were hired for work that was more than menial. But we did not feel welcome there. One day, at the beginning of our break after we left the floor, a White woman turned to me and said, 'Can you make some tea for us?' Although the words were innocuous, I understood that this was a demand, not a question.

"I immediately answered, 'No. I'm not making you tea.' The White woman backed down and never spoke to me again. I had been hired to do the same job she was doing, not to make tea, clean the toilets, or anything else. We were all the same age, were at the same education level, were all hired to do the same job. But in their minds, I was Black and therefore only fit to make their tea. I refused."

After graduating high school, Mom went to the University of Zululand with plans to become an attorney. She was required to attend that university, not Turfloop University as she desired, because that was the one designated for Blacks whose mother tongue was Zulu—even though it was in another state, far from Soweto, and she spoke Sotho just as well as she spoke Zulu. Mom was very politicized and determined to see all people enjoy equal rights, including the right to choose where to study rather than being forced to attend the university for "your kind," especially considering that the universities for the various "your kinds" were run on very tight budgets, while the universities for Whites were given so much more. During her first year, Mom was elected to the Student Representative Council, and in her second year was one of the leaders of a student protest against inferior conditions on campus. The protest was supposed to have been limited to skipping classes and holding rallies on campus, but things got out of hand, and there was some violence at times. When Mom and some others staged a protest rally at the home of the university rector, who was Black, he refused to come out and hear their demands. This protest broke up without any violence, but the university decided to close the campus for two weeks.

Back home, Mom bleached a pair of jeans and wrote "Black Rage" on them. She then went into Johannesburg and walked around in her protest jeans, practically daring all who saw to debate her. She wanted to be confrontational; she wanted the Whites to see that Blacks were angry. "Doing this was subversive, but I didn't care. I wanted the Whites to know that I was angry!"

She dropped out of university and, in 1975, went to work for a large clothing company called Edgars Group. Well-known in South Africa, Edgars owned a few retail chains, including Edgars Stores, which were targeted at White customers, and Sales House and Jet Stores, which were targeted at Blacks and Coloureds. Mom worked at Edgars' headquarters, performing merchandising duties in the buying department. Once the company buyers had decided which lines of clothing to purchase for the various stores, the merchandisers were responsible for getting the items into the stores, making sure they were displayed properly, shifting inventory from stores where they were not selling well to stores where they were, and so on. Although Mom was not a merchandiser, she was performing merchandising duties.

Sometime after she began working at Edgars, the company announced that Blacks could now be admitted to the buyers-training program. Buyers would travel around the country and sometimes go abroad, visiting fashion shows and manufacturers, talking to people in the business, and otherwise figuring out which lines of clothing should be purchased for the coming season. Being invited to join a training course for buyers was quite a step, for at the time, the position of buyer was reserved for Whites. By law, the job was closed to Blacks. Mom sailed through the course, and when it was complete, she looked forward to being among the first group of Black buyers! It made perfect sense, for up until then, Whites had been buyers for all the Edgars stores, even those catering to Blacks and Coloureds. Surely, Black buyers would understand the needs and tastes of Black customers better than Whites would in heavily segregated South

Africa. After all, most Whites rarely associated with Blacks unless they were housekeepers or other menial workers, so Whites had little understanding of Black fashion tastes.

On graduation day, Mom dressed in her Sunday best and went to company headquarters for the ceremony. It wasn't a huge deal—no families were invited—but it was still very nice, with the graduates, their teachers, the buyers and merchandisers, and other company staff gathered in a large, decorated room. Refreshments had been set out, and as each graduate entered the room, they were greeted by a woman holding a large tray of rosettes. She gave them their rosette, and another woman standing next to her helped them pin it on.

"I looked at my rosette," Mom said, "and it had a little piece of paper on it that said 'Still to Come.' I didn't understand this. 'Still to come?' I said to the two women, 'I'm not still to come. I'm here.'

"I didn't know what this meant, but as I looked at all the rosettes on the tray, I could see that the ones for the Black students all said 'Still to Come.' I talked to other Black students, and we realized what it meant: we were not going to be buyers. We had completed the course, yet while the White students could now be buyers, the Blacks could not. We were 'Still to Come,' whatever that meant.

"I refused to wear the rosette. So did a few other Black graduates, and our refusal made many people unhappy—including the bosses, who were all White. I don't know why this happened because no one spoke to us about this. Not the instructors, not the bosses.

"After graduation, some of the Blacks, including me, were 'promoted' to merchandiser. We had been doing the work of a merchandiser all along, but now it was official. We were the first group of Black merchandisers—not buyers, merchandisers. Although we were bitterly disappointed that we didn't get to qualify as buyers, we were given brand-new company cars. Was this to console us for what had happened? I don't know. We didn't refuse them, though, because we could use them after work for ourselves."

In the 1980s, after working for Edgars for some years, Mom took a job as a merchandiser with a large shoe company called Dodos. She worked from her desk in the main office in a semi-open area with several other desks, and every day at ten in the morning and three in the afternoon, the "tea lady" would come by.

Many South African companies had a tea lady who went through the offices at various times during the day, pushing a trolley containing cups, spoons, and ingredients for making tea and coffee. She went to each person, asked how they would like their tea or coffee, and prepared and served it. The tea lady was almost always Black, and that was considered a decent job, although there was absolutely no chance of being promoted to anything else.

My mother told me what happened one day. "Rose, the tea lady, had been serving me and the others for quite a while. One day, she skipped my desk, passed me by, and went to serve the next person. I thought she forgot me so I said, 'Rose, where's mine?'

"She said, 'No, you're going to make yourself tea.'

"I was surprised because she made tea for everyone. I said, 'I'm not going to make myself tea. You are employed to make the tea.'

"Then Rose said, 'Who do you think you are?' and slapped me across the face!

"I just sat at my desk, astonished. I didn't cry. I didn't say anything. I didn't go to management, because Black people did not do that then as we didn't expect to be protected. Other people saw what happened, and maybe this was surfaced to management, but they didn't say or do anything. They didn't seek me out or intervene.

"That evening, I visited my parents and told my father what had happened. I often told him about ugly things that happened to me, and he always told me to rise above the pettiness of other people, to remember that no matter how ugly they get, I must maintain my dignity. But this time, he insisted that I tell him the name of the big boss. And the next day, my father went to Dodos without an appointment to see the big boss, Mr. Ralph Dodo. He told Mr. Dodo what had happened and demanded that Rose be fired. Instead, they agreed that Rose would apologize to me, which she did. I accepted her apology, and there was never a problem again.

"I don't know why Rose refused to serve me that day. She had been doing it all along, but perhaps she now felt she was subservient to another Black person and couldn't tolerate that.

"What I do know is that I learned an important lesson from my father that day. He had always taught me to demand my dignity, which I tried to do, but I would never have thought of doing what he did.

"To walk into a White-owned, top-tier company and demand to see the White boss who you did not know—and without an appointment—was very daring in those days. But my father was an unusual man. He was charismatic, confident, and dignified. He spoke forcefully and clearly. He projected an attitude of 'I shall be heard' that generated respect in others, even in racist Whites. And he would not back down; he would insist people listen to him. This surprised the Whites and made some of them respect him enough that they would hear what he had to say.

"Most Black people at that time would say to themselves, 'Who would listen to me?' and not even try. But my father believed he was worth listening to and that people of all races had no choice but to treat him with the respect he had for himself.

"I was extremely proud of my father that day. He fought for me. And from then on, I got more respect from the company. I could see and feel it in the little things—such as the tone in which I was addressed was different, more respectful. Nobody ever said anything to me about what happened, but the change was clear."

Some years later in the late 1980s, Mom was working at BMW. This job came about in an unusual way. As you'll learn in a later chapter, my grandfather had struck a deal with BMW to open a car dealership in Soweto, making him the only Black owner of such a dealership. Unfortunately, my grandfather passed away soon after the deal was consummated, and my mother wound up running the dealership for a while with her husband David Ndlovu. As financial conditions were not good for Black people then, the dealership failed. This was unfortunate, and BMW was perfectly within its rights to cancel the deal at this point. However, some of the people handling the closure were less than polite and empathetic, perhaps because Mom was Black, so she wrote a letter to the then-managing director of BMW South Africa, Mr. Hendrik von Kuenheim, and pointed this out. She was complaining about the less-than-dignified treatment she received, not the fact that the dealership had to be closed, and to its credit, BMW replied. Mr. von Kuenheim invited Mom to his office for coffee. Mom calmly pointed out where the problem was, and during the conversation, she mentioned that now that the dealership had been liquidated, she would not be able to pay my private school fees. Mr. von Kuenheim said, "Let me see if there is something I can do about that." Later, Mom received a call from him saying that my fees at Sacred Heart would be taken care of through high school graduation, and he offered her a job as a departmental coordinator.

This act demonstrated BMW's progressive attitude, concern for others, and generosity. They could have ignored Mom, for she was just a Black woman, and Black women were on the absolute bottom of the South African racial ladder. But BMW didn't. This also speaks to the importance of demanding your dignity. Mom had learned well the lessons her father had taught her and thought enough of herself to believe that her voice was worth hearing. Rather than accepting the apartheid story that Blacks were inferior—rather than simply fearing the "White man"—she spoke up for herself. And in this case, she was rewarded for doing so.

After Mom had worked for BMW for several years, she told the company that she wished to complete her university education to become an attorney. They offered her funding on the condition that she return to work for them once she graduated, and when she completed law school, BMW arranged for her to do her "articles" at one of the law firms that handled their business. Doing your articles is the equivalent of an internship—the period during which you learn the practical aspects of being an attorney under the guidance of established lawyers, gain experience and insight by working with them, and gradually take on more complex assignments.

Since Mom was connected with BMW, you would think the attorneys she supported would pay close attention to her in order to please an important client. They didn't. They didn't pay much attention to her at all, treating her with less regard than the White articled clerks (candidate attorneys). As Mom put it, "The White attorneys would make sure the White candidate attorneys understood the nitty gritty of the cases they handled. They would talk to them; take them to court with them all the time. But not so with the Blacks. They would throw stuff at the Black candidate attorneys and say, 'Do this; do that,' or send you to court to make a particular argument in a case. Making a single argument in court isn't nearly as good as working your way through a case from beginning to end, learning how the attorneys conceptualize it, prepare it, handle setbacks, and so on. Most of the learning takes place when you shadow an attorney all the way through a case, not when you're just told to go here and file this paper; go there and make that argument. The White attorneys wanted to empower the White candidate attorneys with this knowledge, but not the Black ones."

You might be surprised that the attorneys she supported deliberately ignored and underprepared my mother. Surely, they didn't want her returning to her employer and telling them what a crummy experience she'd had there! Even if they were racist, shouldn't they have at least pretended to be nice? Not by their thinking. To them—and many other Whites at that time—it was impossible to conceive of a Black person being important enough to make a difference in their lives. It speaks to the mind-set of the time: Blacks are not important. These attorneys undoubtedly believed that even if she managed to become an attorney and work at BMW, no one there would pay any attention to her. And in a very real sense, they were right because, for a very long time (including in my days), Black people didn't matter. Many Black South Africans have reported suffering through the same sort of neglect during and after their internships at predominantly White public accounting and law firms. I also experienced this.

"Back then," my mother explained, "Blacks were supposed to take on the inferiority complex; were supposed to believe they were less than others. Blacks who had a healthy view of themselves—however they showed it—were thought to be arrogant, even threatening. In my parents' time, even in my time, it was very surprising to see a Black person demand respect.

"Back then, many if not most Blacks were so run over they didn't speak up. Part of it was our culture, for among Black people, children were to be seen and not heard. In your own household, you were not encouraged to express your opinions. Then in the workplace, the apartheid system forced you to keep quiet and take whatever you were given—and if you didn't, you were punished—so not expressing an opinion almost came naturally to Blacks at the time. We were muzzled. But I wouldn't be muzzled if it meant surrendering my dignity. And I wouldn't let other people's ugly behavior harm me."

That attitude—be strong, be dignified, and don't let others drag you down—was passed through Mom to me. I remember the time when I was about ten years old, and the neighborhood kids had been teasing me about having a boyfriend. I didn't have one but was stung by this and went to my mother, expecting her to hug me and tell me everything would be all right. Instead, she simply said, "And?" Meaning, "And why are you letting what people say upset you?"

Her response to many of my childhood complaints and cries for help was "And?" or "So?" for that was what she had been taught by Mamkhulu. When I was at Sacred Heart, we brought our physical training, or PT, clothes with us to school in a separate bag. Sometimes, my classmates would forget their bags, so they would call home, and their mothers would bring the bags to them within the half hour. Mind you, these were mostly White kids whose mothers did not work and lived fairly near the school. One day, I forgot my PT bag and called my mother at her work. When I told her my tale of woe and asked her to bring my PT bag, she responded by asking, "And what do you expect me to do? It's up to you to remember the things you need to do." Today, I understand that she didn't have the luxury of telling her boss that she had to leave work because her daughter forgot something. That kind of latitude just wasn't extended to Blacks then. So now I understand that she couldn't allow me to become dependent on others, not even on her, for I had to learn to stand on my own two feet. The best she could do was to insist that I develop the habit of remembering what needed to be remembered, getting to where I needed to go, and doing what I needed to do. She was teaching me that as a Black woman under apartheid, I was alone. Yes, I was part of a loving family and part of a larger community, but there was a very sharp limit to what they could do for me. If I wanted to rise up and out of the "Soweto life," I would have to learn to look to myself.

Learning to Stand My Ground on My "Own"

Until the age of eleven, it was perfectly natural to me to see families with two parents, some children, a grandparent, and a distant relative or two sharing a three-room house. Not a three-bedroom house, a three-*room* house with exactly one bedroom, one kitchen, and one living room—plus the toilet in the back yard. The fact that I was an only child sharing a three-room house with only my two grandparents and one uncle—and later with just my grandmother—made me an oddity. When it was four of us in the house, I slept on the uncarpeted floor in my grandparents' bedroom with two blankets laid down every night to serve as my mattress, and Trevor slept on two blankets of his own laid next to mine. Later, when it was mostly just Mamkhulu and I, we shared the double-sized bed in the bedroom; when Trevor was around, he slept in the living room. Sharing a bed was a lot better than sleeping on the floor, as so many residents of Soweto did.

As far as I knew, sleeping on the floor, peeing in a pot, dealing with street crime, and living in cramped homes was simply the way things things were for the majority of us then. I didn't know anything but poverty and failed attempts at trying to get ahead. There were exceptions, of course, but I'm speaking in general terms.

Looking back, I realize there was one thing I knew—and knew well—which helped me believe there was something more for me: that was the Langa women's practice of being introspective, of asking themselves what they could do better. Khokho looked around at her community and saw how it was sinking lower and lower. That was not surprising, given that apartheid worked so hard to strip us of our humanity. But she was determined not to devolve. Instead, she encouraged her children, grand-children, and great-grandchildren to read, and she made it a point to take care of herself. She dressed well and groomed her hair, even though there was no point in doing so. After all, it wouldn't get her a better life, a job, or a promotion. But she still took care of herself for her own sense of self-worth. She was so stylish that the lady of the family for whom she worked used to say, "Gertrude, you're a beauty without paint." But doing her job well and taking care of herself didn't earn her more money or a promotion, for neither was available to her. Still, she was determined to maintain her dignity and self-esteem, and to continually ask herself what she could do to better herself or her children.

Evolving Responses

Langa women have a history of not crying. It's not that we don't feel pain—we do. It's only natural to feel hurt when you're denigrated, stripped of your humanity, and maligned. It's just as natural to want to wallow in that pain or to hit back. But we have learned that neither self-pity nor unrestrained anger is fruitful. Rather than crying, or striking out in anger, we strive to make the best choices given our circumstances. We choose instead to forgive, and to take a step back so we can figure out how best to move forward.

That's why Khokho's response to apartheid was "Don't cry, maintain your self-esteem, and learn from others. Look around you and decide what you need to avoid. Don't worry if others criticize you for doing so."

Mamkhulu's response to apartheid was "Don't cry; comply. Do what it takes to survive."

Mom's response to apartheid was "Don't cry, and don't capitulate. Demand your dignity."

My response to apartheid has been "Don't cry, and always strive to fight for your dignity, but do so on the basis of humanity rather than race."

Shortly after I was born, my mother wrote this about me in her journal: "She has arrived, the liberator of the people." Mom was a highly politicized twenty-two-year-old when she wrote that, and this was at a high point in the struggle. She had embraced the ethos of the Black Consciousness Movement and its many slogans, which promoted Black pride and elevated Blacks while sometimes denigrating Whites. Back then, before she became a born-again Christian, she viewed Whites as the enemy: as she understood it, they were hell-bent on making the lives of Black people miserable. She was a fighter and wanted me to be one, too.

"We were battling for our freedom, our survival," she told me. "When I wrote that, I was thinking you would carry on from where we left off. If whatever dent in apartheid we made was not sufficient, then you, the next generation, would make dents of your own."

Mom, who thought of herself as a fighter, wanted to raise me to be a fighter. And I do see myself as a fighter, but as one fighting a different fight. Mom *had* to fight for survival and dignity for herself, for me, and for Black people. Thanks to her, to my other forebears, and many more like them, apartheid has fallen, and although South Africa has a long way to go, the battleground has changed. The fight is now—or now should be—about healing wounds and bringing the various groups together to build a future in which all can prosper emotionally, physically, and financially. It should be about remembering and honoring the past, but not letting it prevent South Africa from moving forward. It should be about looking beyond skin color, accent, cultural background, and all the rest, in order to see one's neighbor as a human being.

Apartheid stripped tens of millions of people of dignity, humanity, and the right to self-determination on an individual and collective basis.

Though I am now living thousands of miles from South Africa and have embraced the US as my home, I want to see these precious items returned to *all* people, no matter what race they may be.

The Next Step Is…?

The response to apartheid and racism has evolved through four generations of Langa women, and now there is a new generation: my two daughters. Although they were born after apartheid fell and are being raised in a nice, clean, safe suburb in the United States, they have been affected by what happened. It's impossible for them not to be, especially as they grow older and learn more about the life that was inflicted upon their mother, grandparents, great-grandparents, and all their other maternal ancestors going back to the arrival of the first Dutch settlers in South Africa in the 1600s. And they have already been affected by the scars—known and unknown—that I bear.

Not only have my daughters been affected by apartheid, but they may also struggle with the issue of race in the United States. With a White father and a Black mother, they are of mixed race. Although they are young, and our predominantly White community is, in my experience, very racially progressive, my girls may eventually be forced to grapple with the lingering after-effects of slavery, Jim Crow, and the fact that race-related issues continue to form part of the political discourse.

They may feel rejection from some Whites who will say that they are really Black, and rejection from some Blacks who will say they are not Black enough. They may feel pressure to deny part of their heritage and to cling fast to one "side" or the other. Or perhaps they may struggle with the feeling of not belonging at all. My son may also wrestle with these issues.

I want only the best for my three children, and to my mind, that includes teaching them to be strong and helping them develop the strength to not break down when faced with challenging situations or when treated unfairly or oppressively by others, should that happen. But I wonder how they will complete that concept: "Don't cry," and what else?

I can't say which "what else" each of them will choose. I can't even say which they *should* choose, for life on Mercer Island in the State of Washington today is nothing like life was in Soweto, and life as a person of mixed race in the United States today is nothing like life was in South Africa back then.

And who knows? Maybe they'll find, as I expect, that their part of the world here is so much better, enough so that it's perfectly acceptable for the descendants of Langa women to cry once in a while. So long as they don't let their emotions overtake their reason and ability to take a step back, forgive, and choose the best path forward, I'm okay with that.

CHAPTER THREE

I'm Not Your "Kaffir," Not Your Toyi-Toying "Comrade"

Growing up, I loved knowing that I represented almost all that is "Black" in the South African context and that this was evident in my birth names: Tebogo Lindiwe Langa. "Tebogo"—a Setswana name meaning "we are thankful"—was given to me by my father's side of the family, who are of the Molewa clan, a Pedi-speaking people with (we believe) Venda tribal roots. "Lindiwe"—which is Zulu for "one who is expected or awaited for"—was given to me by my mom's Zulu- and Swazi-speaking side of the family. My maiden name, "Langa," derived from my maternal grandfather, means "sun" in Zulu, though the members of my grandfather's clan were Pedi-speaking Ndebeles.

I loved knowing that my ancestors represented many threads in the South African tribal tapestry, and that to them, "ethnicity" was only a part of their makeup; it did not rigidly define who they were. My immediate ancestors didn't only associate with their "kind." Instead, they eagerly stepped across ethnic divides to tie the knot with those not quite as they were, and they were just as comfortable to speak in Pedi or Sotho as they were to speak in Zulu. For them, language was just a means of communication and not something that defined the essence of who they were. I knew they viewed their cultural makeup as evolving, not static, and I was proud of this. When people would ask me "What are you?," as they were so inclined to do, I would always proudly reply, "I'm Black," instead of saying, "I'm Pedi." (According to Black tradition, a child's ethnicity follows the father's lineage, which would make me Pedi.) Whenever they would go on to ask "But are you Zulu or Sotho or what?," I would always quip, "I'm everything Black," and then name all my ethnic strands. For me, the issue under apartheid wasn't so much about who I was genealogically speaking, but rather who I was intrinsically. It was about how I chose to define myself in the face of forces that were intent on bending my identity to fall in line with their own desires.

Looking back as I'm writing this, it feels odd to speak of having exercised choice back then, given that Blacks had so few choices due to a number of statutes that were enacted, which, in some respects, mirrored the Jim Crow laws that were passed here in the United States. We could not freely choose where to live, for we were restricted to either the "Bantustans"[5] or a township such as Soweto. We could not freely choose which public schools to attend, for we had to go to the ones that provided a separate system of education for Blacks—separate and inherently inferior, by design—than that offered to Whites. Our choice of jobs was severely limited, with all the important and well-paying ones reserved for others. We didn't have the right to decide when to be in or travel through cities, thanks to the "Pass Laws" that were not repealed until ten years after I was born. We could not freely choose whom to marry, for wedlock across racial lines was strictly forbidden, just as it was here in the United States before these "anti-miscegenation laws" were finally struck down by the Supreme Court in 1967. Even our choice of a final resting place was severely restricted. We did have one undisputed "right," though, which was to live on a Bantustan, a piece of land that had been reserved for your tribe—but only the one granted to your native tribe, for lands given to other tribes were off-limits to you. Apartheid said that the indigenous

Black tribes were separate and distinct, making a point to emphasize our differences by setting up separate lands for many of us, each under the "rule" of a tribal chief. Four years before I was born, this culminated with a statute that formally designated us as citizens of one or another of the Bantustans. It declared that we were "aliens" in urban areas and, therefore, were only allowed to live in urban areas if we had special permission. This statute included those of us who were already—and had long been—living in townships in the so-called "White South Africa."

From the 1960s through the 1980s, the Bantustan system was bolstered by a program of forced removals, which saw millions of Blacks ripped away from their homes and dumped in the Bantustans. Sometimes, when urban areas such as Sophiatown were "cleaned-up" before the land was given over to the Whites, the displaced Blacks were pushed into Soweto. Due to these forced removals, at one point, the Whites—who constituted about fifteen percent of the population then—owned more than eighty percent of South African land.

As if that were not enough, the apartheid government worked very hard to define us as the lowest of the low, occupying the bottom-most rung on the ladder of racial-seniority classification, deserving of no more than crumbs falling off White, Indian, and Coloured tables. And it wasn't just that we actually had so much less; it was that the system sought to condition us from birth to believe that we were grossly inferior specifically because we were Black, with cruel slurs such as *kaffir* liberally used to refer to us. The word *kaffir* is derived from Arabic for "non-believer," but in the South African context it took on a derogatory significance, very much like the word *nigger*.

The architects of apartheid desperately wanted to shape my identity, at the core of which was the idea that I was an "ignorant, thieving, lazy, lying kaffir."

In addition, apartheid pushed Blacks to identify strongly as members of a particular tribe, trying to enforce the divisions by, among other measures, dividing Soweto into various zones based on tribal language. Though tribal division had long existed, the government went to great lengths to strengthen the divisions so as to keep us from joining together and demanding our freedom and dignity.

Early in life, I wondered how I could embrace the tribal narrative, given my rich multiethnic heritage and the fact that we didn't adhere to any traditional tribal customs. My family did not feel connected to any of the Bantustans. With such diversity in our makeup, which one could we fully feel was "ours"? Within Soweto, my grandparents lived in the predominantly Zulu-speaking Orlando East, while my parents lived in Naledi, where Sotho was the more common language. As a family, we were just as comfortable in Orlando East as we were in Naledi. We were making up our identity and culture as we went along; we were ethnically diverse Sowetans and loved it. I rejected the idea that I had to be a particular "kind" of Black person, and I utterly rejected the larger apartheid narrative that Blacks were inferior.

Up until the age of eleven, I had hardly any contact with White people, or those of any other "race," for that matter.[6] In accordance with the Group Areas Act, which strictly separated Whites, Indians, Coloureds, and Blacks, I lived in an all-Black township in Orlando East and attended an all-Black private school called St. John Berchman's, which was just down the road from my grandmother's house. In truth, I didn't give much thought to Whites—or other races, for that matter—until I began preparing to switch to a mixed-race private Catholic school called Belgravia Convent. As I said earlier, this was one of the relatively few schools to flout apartheid by allowing the racial groups to mix, offering a good education to all. When some of my Black classmates heard I was going to apply to this school, they told me that it would be very difficult to get in, for it was run by Whites and I would be competing with White students. "White people are very intelligent," they told me.

Sadly, some of my friends had already internalized feelings of Black inferiority. I didn't know if Whites were truly more intelligent—and by implication, better than me—for I hadn't had any exposure to them. But these friends, only ten years old or so, already "knew" that they were inferior. Fortunately, I was at the top of my class at St. John Berchman's, and

I aced the Belgravia entrance exam, scoring high enough to avoid having to repeat a year, which is what usually happened when a student shifted from a Black school to a White-run, White-majority private school.

I might have internalized the narrative that Whites are naturally superior but for three things. First, that attitude never resonated with me because I learned at home that I have value and that it was up to me to determine how others should treat me. From the time I was a little girl, my mother, Esther Happy Langa, would say to me, "Lindi, you have an invisible sign on your back, and people can read it. This sign tells people what you think of yourself and how you want to be treated. If your sign says, 'I'm worth a million dollars,' that's how people will treat you." She was teaching me that if I wrote "I deserve respect" on my sign, not only would others respond accordingly, but I would be reinforcing my belief in myself.

Second, I was fortunate enough to mix with kids of all racial backgrounds, from age eleven right through high school graduation. Having done so, I understand why apartheid tried so hard to keep us apart, for the simple act of interacting with the "others" allowed me to let go of the misconceptions and outright lies spewed out by apartheid. I discovered that we are all human beings with more or less similar aspirations and talents. I, a Black person, performed well academically and was in the honors class for the greater part of my years in middle and high school. Likewise, my cousin Reitumetse Langa clinched first place every year at Belgravia Convent. During my years at Belgravia Convent and Sacred Heart, I served as a house captain, dormitory leader, and captain of the netball team—all amid student populations that were largely White. My fellow Sacred Heart students elected me to the Student Representative Council, from whence I was elected to the Executive Committee of the Student Representative Council. I was later elected by the student body to be one of the two Sacred Heart representatives to the Johannesburg Junior City Council, a local student governance body comprised of learners from predominantly White government schools all over Johannesburg. I was the only Black person, if not the only person of color, in the council of some eighty or more students.

The point is not that I'm so wonderful, for many students ranked higher than I did academically, ran circles around me on the sports field, or were better leaders. The point is that when we were treated as equals we performed as equals, and as willing partners and friends. The school operated as a meritocracy. We were expected to perform and almost every student did so, regardless of background.

Third, the Sacred Heart leadership—headed by Brother Neil McGurk and later, after I graduated, by Mr. Stephen Lowry—was deeply committed to the idea of building a nonracial community in which all scholars were treated according to their character rather than their skin color. Indeed, Sacred Heart brazenly defied apartheid by allowing students of various races to mix freely; endured desecration of school property by state security forces; helped White students avoid military conscription; trained students to respond to bomb threats on campus; literally hid Eric Molobi, Frank Chikane, and other Black resistance leaders on school premises; and accomplished even more as part of our campaign for equality.

In high school, one of my classmates, Antalene Jordaan, occasionally organized a "movie Saturday," wherein several of us of various races would go to the movies together, crossing race lines as if it was the most natural thing in the world. It wasn't, of course—not in apartheid South Africa— and we drew attention because it was so rare to see mixed groups in those days when apartheid was still in force, even if weakening. One time, a White bus driver refused to let a Black student from my school onto a public bus, for the bus was reserved for Whites, Indians, and Coloureds. Our classmates who happened to be boarding at the same time as this student then refused to get on, out of solidarity with him. When this incident was shared by school leaders during our morning school assembly the next day, we all felt so proud of what these students had done and so proud of our school for inculcating a culture of equality and zero tolerance for discrimination.

Being judged by the content of my character rather than by the color of my skin was thrilling. That's not to say it was easy, however, because we came from different worlds. Starting at age eleven, I came into daily contact with kids who took it for granted that they would succeed, would graduate from university to go on to rewarding careers. This was at a time when I could hardly dream of graduating from high school, let alone achieving more—this just wasn't done in my neighborhood. Not only were my horizons set low by apartheid, but I lacked general knowledge of the outside world, influential family connections, and everything else. But I pushed on because I wanted to do well and because so many teachers at school—most of them White—spurred me on. They helped me believe that maybe, just maybe, I could succeed despite apartheid. Interacting with teachers and fellow students at Belgravia Convent and Sacred Heart helped me kick aside the apartheid-engendered lie that I was doomed to fail solely because of my race. That, combined with the support I received from my family and my trust in God, ultimately led me to believe that with faith and hard work, I could overcome.

But even as my family, teachers, and classmates were encouraging me to broaden my horizons and try to expand my options, there was pressure to restrict my choices coming from those who associated themselves with the anti-apartheid movement. I was in school during the height of the anti-apartheid resistance, with resistance leaders seeking to define the norms and attitudes that people of color should adopt in an effort to build a successful coalition against the system. Beginning in the late 1980s, there was tremendous pressure to engage in anti-apartheid, anti-establishment strikes, "stay-aways" from work, and class boycotts. Spurred by the cry, "Liberation first, education later," sixty thousand students stayed away and eighty schools were closed down in 1980. Five years later, when I was in grade seven, six hundred and fifty thousand students boycotted!

I was uncomfortable with this pressure, feeling like the resistance "leaders" wanted me to be a rebel soldier or comrade, as they defined the term, marching and *toyi-toying* to their beat. The *toyi-toyi* was the dance of the protest movement, an energetic jogging or jumping from one foot to the other to the rhythm of the "leader," who shouted out the demands. Everyone else chanted in response, pumping their fists in the air. The chant often ended with everyone jumping from one foot to the other while chanting "*hayi hayi*," which means "no, no" or "no ways, no ways." In other words, no way will we accept this oppressive apartheid regime. Many times—too many to count—huge groups of protesters *toyi-toyed* down the street to a government building, where they danced and chanted their anguish. Sometimes the government responded with silence, sometimes with bullets.

While I fully understood the need for protest as well as the desire for the community to be united against apartheid, I felt it was even more important to be educated—even if, at that time, the lives of educated Blacks were only marginally better than those of the uneducated. I felt it was important to have a chance, no matter how small, to improve my life in hopes that this would be more beneficial to the community down the road. I also felt that it should be up to me to decide how I wanted to respond to the atrocities of apartheid. I disliked the feeling that some people were seeking to rob me of my power to choose my response, and that they insisted on making decisions for me purely because we happened to be linked by race.

I didn't want to be forced to identify myself as a school-skipping "*toyi-toying* comrade" any more than I wanted to be required to see myself as a "kaffir."

My Identity? I'm Me!

To this day, my identity is hard to pigeonhole. If I had to categorize it, I'd simply say that I am "cosmopolitan." Twenty or so years back, a close friend accused me of being a "chameleon," implying that I needed to "be something," to firm up my identity by acting in a particular way or maybe by aligning with a specific culture. I wasn't sure what to make of this, but now I feel that being a chameleon is a gift that allows me to interact and feel at home with people from all corners of the world. Being a chameleon has made it easier to assimilate into the culture of my adopted home country and to pursue a new identity as a patriotic American citizen while holding on to all that is dear to me from my past. South Africa is very dear to me, which is why I want to see the country prosper. I happen to be a Black woman, yes, but I am also a Christian, a mother, a lawyer, a Seattle Opera season ticket holder, a hockey fan (go Bruins!), a tennis enthusiast, a Shakespeare devotee, a former Goth and G&R fan, a sushi junkie, a fashionista, a lover of Ndebele art, a brand-new and somewhat nervous student of Hebrew, and so much more. In other words, I am a unique human being with all the strengths, weaknesses, fears, and hopes that make one human. That is how I wish to be treated. And that is how I wish to treat others. While recognizing and respecting the culture inherited from my forebears, I want to keep exploring and, in so doing, continually refresh and enrich my life.

In 2003, I married Matt, a White man from the United States who traces his family line mainly back to Europe (France, Scotland, and Ireland), so our three children are "mixed race." In South Africa, even though the term "Black" has been broadened to include Indians and Coloureds, they would be identified as Coloured, but in the United States, there is no such category. In fact, it is considered by many here to be an offensive term. Although my children are Americans, I'm trying to teach them about all the strands of their heritage and let them decide for themselves who they intrinsically are. Most of all, I don't want them to allow others to dictate how they should be defined.

If we were living in South Africa, people would identify my children as being different and ask about their heritage. Indeed, when we were living in South Africa, some people asked me if the babies I was holding were mine, as they were quite fair-skinned when they were very young. The people asking these questions weren't being mean. It's just that race is still a major issue in South Africa and people are curious. It's in the air. But where we've lived in the United States, nobody has asked. I see this as one of the factors indicating how progressive we are as a country. Needless to say, the 2017 white nationalist rally, counter-protest, and death of a protester in Charlottesville, Virginia, show that there are some issues yet to work out—as well as some rather odd quirks. For example, when I initially registered my children at school, I was asked to fill out various forms, one of which asked about ethnicity. You could check the box for "Black" or the box for "White" or several other boxes, but there was no box for "Mixed." I didn't want to only recognize one part of their heritage, so I thought I'd check both "Black" and "White." The instructions explained that if you did not select a category, someone from the school would choose it for you, based on observation.

I laugh when I think of that, because in the bad old days of apartheid, many people were indeed classified by others on the basis of observation.

I wonder, *How would my kids do on the pencil test?*[7]

What's the Sign on Your Back?

How we see ourselves and the value (if any) we ascribe to ourselves is a very complex issue. We are often pushed in various directions by our families, ethnic culture, gender, religion, socioeconomic status, and other factors. Ultimately, though, where we land on this should be up to us. My mom encouraged me to see myself as valuable. She wanted me to choose to see myself in the best light possible, in defiance of how apartheid's architects, racists, tribalists, sexists, and those with nefarious intentions saw me. I chose to see myself as more than a kaffir, Pedi, *isifebe*, or potential *toyi-toyer*. I also chose to give others the opportunity to show me how they wanted me to define them. Unfortunately, this wasn't always reciprocated. I found that people often projected their own perception of my identity on me, and that they did this to others as well. This is the subject of the next chapter.

CHAPTER FOUR

CAN THEY TAKE MY
BLACKNESS AWAY?

D etermined to continue my education after graduating from high
school in 1991, I enrolled in the Bachelor of Commerce program
at the University of the Witwatersrand (Wits). Like South African ele-
mentary and high schools, which were segregated in 1953, the nation's
universities were segregated by law in 1959. The prestigious universities
had been reserved for Whites, and these institutions were allotted far
more resources than the others. Meanwhile, Indians and Coloureds were
assigned to "their" university. The situation was more complex for Blacks,
who were further divided by tribe. For instance, Zulu-speakers or those
classified as Zulu were required to attend Zululand University, while
Sothos were required to attend Turfloop.

There was an exception to this rule back then: "others" could petition
to attend a White university if they could demonstrate that their desired
course of study was not offered at the universities designated for their
group. A small number of waivers were granted every year, but the fortunate few to whom they were given were restricted to just a few courses of
study at the White universities.

Some historically White universities, including Wits, had vigorously protested against this educational segregation. In 1957, when the apartheid government was indicating that it wanted to establish segregated universities, Wits and three other universities issued a statement called "The Open Universities in South Africa," which affirmed their commitment to academic freedom and desire to educate all who wished to learn. Two thousand academic staff members, students, and alumni marched from Wits to the Johannesburg City Hall behind a banner reading "Against Separate Universities Bill." But they were forced to back down and become nearly-all-White institutions. Wits did, however, remain at the forefront of the anti-apartheid movement, bending apartheid rules so as to allow in as many "others" as possible.

In 1987, Wits defied the apartheid government by declaring itself open to educating all. The government responded with anger, arresting, banning, and deporting students and staff, and often sending police swarming onto the campus to disrupt protest meetings—even protests that were peaceful. By the time I arrived in 1992, apartheid was breathing its last and this law had been repealed. But while Wits was now officially open to all, it was far from being fully integrated. Although Blacks constituted about eighty percent of the South African population back then, when I walked onto the campus in 1992, the student body was sixty-four percent White and only about twenty-two percent Black, twelve percent Indian, and two percent Coloured.[8] Even though the number of "others" was slowly rising, the races generally did not mix much socially. Students pretty much self-segregated in the classrooms, residence halls (called "res" or "dorms," for dormitory), and elsewhere. Even parties held in the res were segregated, with a "razzle" as a party for Whites and a *"gumba"* as one for Black students. There were no regulations enforcing this separation, but with few exceptions, the unofficial segregation was so strict that there may as well have been. The races even belonged to different student government organizations, with Whites supporting one group and Blacks another. These groups only merged to constitute a nonracial Student Representative Council a year or so before I joined. This de facto segregation was quite ironic, for at that time, Wits was considered the most racially progressive university in the nation, and for those who came from segregated high schools, it probably was.

The Wits faculty was generally dedicated and progressive. But since both faculty and administration had mostly been appointed during apartheid, they were overwhelmingly White. Waiting for these professors and administrators to retire and be replaced with a new set more closely matching the South African demographics would take decades. That was far too long for groups such SASCO (South African Students Congress). They wanted the university to "transform" and become more Black on every level—student composition, faculty, and administration—right away! They also wanted the university to provide more financial assistance to Black students. SASCO was strongly committed to the idea that the transformation must be led by Black people, not Whites. So despite the fact that Wits had long championed the educational rights of all people of color while still maintaining its ability to deliver a great education, it was seen as not progressive enough because its leaders were primarily White. SASCO wanted it to become something very different, practically overnight. And they weren't going to sit back and wait for the change.

I learned this firsthand as a member of student government. In 1993, as a second-year student, I ran for and won a place on the Commerce Students' Council, which represented students to the Commerce Faculty, about ninety percent of whom were White. Of the ten members of the council, the majority were White, and seven were male. They elected me council president, which, to the best of my knowledge, made me the first Black president of a university faculty council in the history of Wits. As president of the Commerce Council, I automatically became a member of the All-Faculty Council, and the members of this council elected me to be one of their two representatives on the Wits Senate Committee, one of the highest decision-making bodies on campus.

As a member of the governing bodies of Wits, I found myself caught up in the struggle to "transform" Wits. And what a struggle it was, with SASCO staging frequent, raucous protest marches through the campus, overturning trashcans, bursting into classrooms to disrupt classes, damaging property, intimidating teachers and students who disagreed with their tactics, and causing enough disruption to impede effective learning for a number of days. The vice-chancellor and principal of the university at the time, Prof. Robert Charlton, authorized the deployment of police on campus and, working with Prof. June Sinclair, the deputy vice-chancellor of student affairs, he went to court to obtain a final interdict (injunction) against SASCO and SASCO WITS. Things came to a head when well over one hundred protestors were arrested in a single day of protest.

While some students agreed with the idea of disrupting or completely shutting down the university to speed up "transformation," others wished to get on with their studies. I felt that SASCO's ends were understandable, but I had serious reservations about their means. Just like I did when I was younger, I believed that the best way to move the needle on such issues was to give Black students a chance to learn, so that the pool of Black professors and staff members who might be qualified to teach at Wits in the future might be increased—or at least allow the students to make their own choices between learning and boycotting. And I made no bones about expressing my opinion.

As head of the Commerce Students' Council, I stood up to speak on the issue at a campus meeting hosted by the Commerce and Engineering Student Councils in the East Campus Amphitheater. My speech was short and to the point:

We are here for an education, regardless of color. Everybody here, regardless of color, is making a substantial investment in themselves and in the future of this country. We cannot, at any cost, jeopardize this. The recent violence on campus is posing a threat to our primary concern.

In view of this, the Commerce Students' Council implores SASCO and the Administration to reassess and resolve the methods employed in resolving the issues at hand in order to create an environment conducive to learning and teaching. We want the best education possible.

On this day of peace, let us commit ourselves to the spirit of reconciliation.

In conclusion, the Commerce Students Council implores all students, Black and White, to cease all hostilities.

Thank you.

Even this little plea to peacefully solve the issues at hand was way too inflammatory for the protestors, and I was shouted down. SASCO members insulted me by calling out "Mangope!" and "Buthelezi!"—these are the names of leaders of two Bantustans who were deemed to have collaborated with the apartheid government. Calling someone a "Mangope" or "Buthelezi" was the equivalent of calling her a "sell out" or an "Uncle Tom." They shouted things like "Sit down, Mangope!" and "You White-man-kitchen-dweller!" throughout my speech. It seemed to me they felt I was not behaving as a Black person "should" and that I was not truly Black.

Upon stepping off the stage, I was quickly surrounded by twenty or so angry SASCO members—all men, towering over me and demanding to know what I had been "going on about" in my speech. It felt so familiar, so much like the almost-jackrolling a few years back. And once again, I chose to hold my ground. One of my fellow committee members, Chris Dykes—who was White—was by my side, and standing nearby were the "peacekeepers," a volunteer group made up of White individuals who were stationed around campus to try to defuse conflict and maintain order. The university felt it was better to turn to these unofficial peace-keepers rather than call in the police, whose mere presence might inflame matters.

As the angry male students were closing their circle around me, Chris and some of the peacekeepers stepped up to my defense, but I quickly asked them to step back. I can't tell you exactly why I did this, for there was no time to think things through—you just react in situations like this and hope you get it right. I guess I was worried that the presence of Chris and the White peacekeepers would raise the tension level. Or maybe it was my experience with the Soweto gangsters and jackrollers kicking in, reminding me it was better to face bullies head-on and alone than to look to others for help. That marked you as being weak, and the next time the bullies wouldn't hesitate to go after you.

I had no plan other than to not back down. Fortunately, I suddenly remembered that I had been at the SASCO office just the other day, going from one person to the next, trying to engage them in discussion about their demands. I was persistent but so were they, and they had perfected the art of not seeing people they didn't want to engage with. Although I was there for quite a while, going from person to person, they did not even acknowledge my presence. I'm really not sure why they did not want to speak to me. Were they put off by my private school accent? Were they wondering why a Black person was looking to understand what their issues were? Did they feel that I should have just been in the know? I have no idea, but I left their office without having been acknowledged or engaged.

"If you disagree with what I said," I began, keeping my voice strong yet neutral, "you had a good opportunity to have 'educated' me when I came to your office the other day to speak to you. Had one of you been willing to at least engage with me, it's possible I might have taken a different stance on this."

They were silent.

They knew I had tried to speak with them and were honest enough to face this truth. They were hoisted by their own petard, convicted by their rude response to me. One by one, they began walking away, mumbling insults under their breath. The matter was not yet closed, however, for over the next several days as I walked past students on East Campus, I would sometimes hear mutters of "*sies*," which is the equivalent of "yuck."

Even "Black" Is a Rainbow

It's very painful to be labeled an "Uncle Tom" or "house negro," or be called other derogatory names. It really hurt me to know that people were questioning my Blackness or challenging that part of my identity. But rather than dwelling on pain, I wanted to focus on making my position known, even when I was surrounded by angry people. Even if I was fighting for my life. Remember, some people like me who were seen as traitors—rightly or wrongly—were "necklaced" back then. They had a car tire jammed over their heads and around their shoulders that was filled with gasoline and set on fire. I was not physically assaulted because we were at Wits with a peacekeeping group and lots of other people standing very close by. Had this confrontation occurred in the township, who knows what might have happened? But I held my ground and said, in effect, "This is what I believe. Whether you agree or not, these are my views, and you do not have the right to determine whether or not I am Black. I *am* Black. My opinion on this issue does not disqualify me from being a person who is Black."

I truly believe that Blackness is not monolithic. Blackness does *not* come in one shade with one common experience, one common thought pattern, one set of aspirations, or even one set of common values. We Black people come in a myriad of shades with a diversity of experiences.

I'm not quite sure how I came to embrace this worldview—common sense, perhaps? Or maybe it was planted in my mind when I was very young, listening to my dad, Thabo Victor Molewa, singing along to Peter Tosh's "African," which speaks to the diversity of the African experience and maintains that Africans are just that: Africans. They are Africans regardless of how dark or fair-skinned they are, where in the world they may happen to live, or which religious denomination they may belong to. Granted, this song speaks to the issue of what it means to be an "African" rather than the South African "Black" experience, but I think I caught the spirit of the message: we should celebrate our diversity of skin tones, perspectives, origins, religious and cultural backgrounds, and experiences, for doing so is a nod to our humanity.

Ironically, those Black people who insisted that all Blacks should act and think alike were behaving like the Whites who sought to oppress us, for they were treating all Blacks as "cutout caricatures" rather than individuals. They were as blind to the variations of experience, thought, and belief within the Black community as was apartheid.

Brutally "Removing His White"

It wasn't only Blacks who were pressured to think and behave in the prescribed manner and were assumed to be doing so just because of their skin color. Some Whites faced the same issue, and in at least one case I know of, things became quite violent. My friend Nic's family was so upset by his marriage to a Black woman named Pauline that they quite literally tried to "take his White away."

Born in 1971, Nic grew up on a family farm in the province of Free State, an agricultural area where most of South Africa's grain is grown. Like many Afrikaner youngsters, Nic played with Black children, the sons and daughters of the Black men and women who lived and worked on the farm. That changed when he began attending school. "My school was White-only and theirs was Black," Nic explained. "We continued playing together on the farm, but this was 1976, and racism was growing. My parents discouraged us from playing with them, and I began picking up on the racism. I would disrespect Black people, not mingle with them, call them the k-word. I didn't treat them as full citizens."

Nic's family belonged to the Dutch Reformed Church and attended services, but it was not until he was twenty-five and was invited by an acquaintance to attend a service at a different church that he truly opened his heart to God. "I thought the service was nice, so when this guy asked me to study the Bible with him and some friends from the church, I did. This was a multiracial church, and I studied the Bible with White and Black brothers and sisters. But I still had racist attitudes. I would not want to greet Black people, eat with them, or share utensils. Some of the brothers I was studying with picked up on this. They challenged me to build friendships with Black people. They pointed out that in God's eyes there is no difference between White and Black people, which meant that I must treat everyone as an equal. They reminded me that all the races will be in heaven, so I could decide if I wanted to be with Black people in heaven or with Black people in hell. I believe the Bible is God's word, so I knew I would be fooling myself if I thought I could get away with treating people poorly just because of their color. Once I made that decision, I began to develop deep friendships with Blacks and others."

Pauline's upbringing was similar to Nic's in that the races were separated, but in her case, it was nearly a total separation. She grew up in a small village called Dipompont outside Pretoria. It was isolated, populated only by Black people, and she only saw people of other races on the rare occasions when she went to town to shop with her mother. Otherwise, Pauline had no interaction with other races whatsoever. "When I was growing up, my parents worked for White people, so the Whites were held in higher esteem than we were. We thought anything White was better, and we resented the Whites and what they had."

Coincidently, Pauline joined the same church Nic did. After matriculating at the age of eighteen, she had moved to Pretoria to pursue further studies in computer science and happened to meet a woman who belonged to this church. Although not terribly interested in religion at the time, Pauline visited the church to see what it was like. "I studied the Bible there and got to know how to interact and build friendships with people I had never interacted with before. It was quite a challenge, but at the same time intriguing. I was challenged to make friends with Whites, to get to know who they were and how they grew up. I came to understand they were human beings like me. The skin color was different, but otherwise, everything else was the same. We are all ultimately the same."

Nic and Pauline met on a church-sponsored hike. He thought she was very attractive, she thought he was sweet, and as Nic says, "We clicked in a way that only God could make happen." Unfortunately, their families were not happy. "My older sister thought I was being stubborn and strange," Pauline explained. "She said, 'It's not like the guy is rich or incredibly good-looking, so what are you trying to achieve?' I wasn't trying to achieve anything; I thought he was sweet.

"This was hard for my dad and mom, because they grew up when

45

apartheid was in full force. The first thing my dad asked was, 'Does he have a gun? If so, he is not a good guy because the Whites are trying to kill the Blacks to reduce the number of people who will vote for Mandela.' I told my dad that Nic was Christian, but he said, 'The people behind apartheid were also Christian.'

"It was very hard for my mother. She had been brutally beaten by the police because she was standing at a 'White Only' bus stop. That happened when she was pregnant with me, and now I was bringing a White man into the house. Not just any White man, but an Afrikaner!

"Some of the people I worked with questioned whether I was really South African or from a different country: How could I date a White guy!? I responded, 'He's my boyfriend and it's not about anything. It is simply that we love each other.'"

Nic's family was also very much against the relationship. His brother told Nic that marrying a Black woman would harm their family, and any children he and Pauline had would be ugly. His father was also very much against the relationship, although Nic recounts, "My mom didn't outright reject it. But she didn't really accept it, either."

Nic and Pauline married in 2000. Although apartheid had fallen six years before, things were still difficult for them. People followed them in the shops, openly talking to each other about how strange it was to see a Black and White person together, holding hands as if they were a couple. And when Pauline, who now had an Afrikaans last name (Janse van Rensburg), went to pick up some medication, the pharmacist and his assistant thought she was a maid fetching the medicines for her "madam."

Shortly after the marriage, when Nic paid a visit to his family, his brother and father took him to a bar for a belated bachelor party. "I was hijacked into this party, and they mistreated me because of who I had become in their eyes. There was my dad, my brother, and some friends. They tried to get me drunk. I wasn't drinking then, but they kept pushing it at me, making fun of me for not drinking it, really going at it. It was a strong rum, and I wound up vomiting it all up.

"Then my brother and some of his friends grabbed me and held me down. I'm physically small, so it was easy for them to do. My brother said, 'If you want to be Black, let's make you Black!' An Afrikaans guy, one of our friends, started to rub a chemical on me while they held me down. This chemical was dying my skin, and he rubbed the chemical on my face and hands. Then they ripped my shirt open to rub it on my chest and back. They said they were going to make me Black.

"I struggled, but couldn't make them stop. Then I looked at the guy who was rubbing the stuff on me, straight in the face, and said, 'Get thee behind me, Satan.'

"He said, 'What? Are you speaking to me?'

"I repeated what I had said.

"He backed off and another guy—a White guy who was English, not Afrikaans—rescued me and took me to the hospital. I spent the night there with chemical burn wounds. I don't remember what my dad was doing, but he wasn't protecting me. From that point on, we separated from my family."

"This was a difficult period," says Pauline. "Luckily, my family was already accepting of Nic. We dated for about a year, and in that time, he visited my parents a lot. My dad got to see what kind of person Nic really is. It got to the point where he could see him as his own son. Then my dad influenced my mom, saying, 'This boy is so innocent, so reliable and honest.' My dad convinced my mom that Nic is the right person for me."

Nic picks up the story: "It was harder with my family. They basically disowned me for three years after the bachelor party. And I knew I had to separate from them to build my relationship with Pauline. The doctor at the hospital suggested I open a legal case against my family, but I thought, *No, God will deal with them.*

"After three years had passed, my dad had a serious health problem and had a leg amputated. We went to visit him, and things started softening up. Eventually, we reconciled. I later learned that we were helped by a friend of my dad's. This was a White man. He had been at the bachelor party and knew what they did. Now he said to my father, 'Part of the reason you are suffering is that you haven't made peace with your son.

He never took revenge on you by filing a case, but you turned your back on him.'

"So God worked in their hearts, and we were reconciled after three years," Nic says. "They realized that Pauline and I love each other. It was important to show them that I valued my marriage more than their opinions, and today, they really love her."

Which Side Is Indian On?

Clearly, there were powerful, pervasive ideas about what it meant to "be Black" or "be White" back then. Many Black people "knew" exactly what a fellow Black should think and how she should act, and were happy to damn her if she didn't. At the same time, many Black people "knew" exactly what Whites were thinking and how they behaved. These Blacks refused to believe Whites could do anything different, and the same was true for many Whites' beliefs about Blacks. These beliefs about "we" and "them" were quite powerful when it came to Blacks and Whites, but less so—at least at Wits—with respect to Indians and Coloureds. The attitudes were there but were not as powerful, perhaps because Indians and Coloureds were seen as "lesser" players in the battle between Black and White.

I have a friend whom I shall call John Paul, an Indian born in India who grew up in South Africa. His family moved there because his parents got jobs as teachers. This was during apartheid, and there were certain neighborhoods where Indians were required to live. But John's family could not live in these areas because they were India-Indian, not South African Indian; they were not accepted by the local Indians and were legally forced to live in a Black township. Therefore, all of young John's friends were Black, and he should have gone to the local Black school with them. But since he didn't speak an African language, which was necessary for going to a Black school, he got special permission to go to school in the Indian area—the one where he couldn't live. The students in this school were nearly all Muslim, with just five Hindu families, and John, the lone Catholic. So John was the Catholic India-Indian living in a Black township and going to the mostly Muslim-Indian school in a South-African-Indian neighborhood, where he wasn't accepted as one of them.

He was, however, the only kid in his school who had ever watched a movie in a movie theater, having gone to a theater with his father in another African country, where they had lived before moving to South Africa. Since the apartheid government did not allow movie theaters for Indians, Coloureds, or Blacks until later, having been to a theater made John unique. Another kid in the school was occasionally allowed to sit in the projection room of a White theater and watch a movie from there because his father was friends with the theater's owner, but John was the only one who had ever sat in the theater itself to watch a movie. John grew up as a total outsider, belonging to no one except his family.

John Paul was at Wits at the same time I was, although I did not know him then. Some of the Indians attending Wits had been to private or international schools and were comfortable mixing with other races, but John—who had little exposure to Whites while growing up—was not. "When I got to Wits, I was nervous, overwhelmed. I was the only kid from my school who went to university that year. Imagine what it was like: you were never exposed to university, never stepped foot on one, and here you are. When you are assigned to a group project, you are the one Indian kid in a group of five or six. You have a sense of identity, and the others have a sense of your identity, and there's a clash. They assume you have no idea what you're talking about because you are Indian and went to inferior schools.

"When I came in 1992, they had just started opening the dorms to kids of color. I lived in the dorms, and there were White kids, Indian kids, and Black kids. It was awkward for me because in some ways, I fit in better with the Black kids than with the Indian kids, and the White kids seemed to be from a different planet. They had a sense of privilege; they expected to be there. They had no struggle to fit in, but coming from an Indian or Black school, you had a sense of being out of your depth.

Remember, I was the only one from my graduating class who went to *any* university that year. You had a sense of being 'not one of them,' even at the parties, the *gumbas* for Blacks or the razzles for Whites.

"So I became a chameleon. I adapted and changed my vocal tone and vocabulary depending on who I was with, so I would be more acceptable to them. Being a chameleon is good in that it allows you to get along with everyone, but you always have this deep, nagging sense within of 'Who am I really?' If you change with every crowd, you wonder who you are on the inside. 'Is being a chameleon my identity? Has it gone from being a skill to being my identity?'

"During the SASCO rioting, I wasn't sure which side to be on. I'm not a SASCO member, but I carried some of the same frustration they did. One morning, SASCO was gathering outside the Great Hall and people were debating what to do. I shouted, 'Let's march into the Great Hall!' People agreed. They shouted, 'Yes!' and marched into the Great Hall, causing havoc.

"I was at the very back of the group as they were rushing into the Great Hall. Someone at the front screamed, 'The police are coming!' and everyone started rushing out. I just stepped aside, sat down on the steps of the Great Hall, and watched this mass of Black kids running out. I'm just sitting there, la-di-da. I'm Indian. No one knows what side I'm on, so the police won't bother me."

John was right. The Black students pouring out of the hall ignored him, as did the police. Apparently, neither the students nor the police identified him as either friend or foe, so they simply ignored him. "Later that afternoon," he continues, "I'm watching, dancing with the protestors, thinking this is cool as they march from building to building and disrupt classes. Then I realize they're going to the hall where the medical classes are, and my then-girlfriend was in one of those. I was happy to disrupt other classes, but not hers. Things could get violent.

"There were peacekeepers around. They wore red bands around their arms and were supposed to be neutral, to just try to help maintain order. I grabbed one of the SASCO banners, which was red, ripped off some material, and tied it around my arm. Then I ran inside the building and began directing the protestors away from my girlfriend's class. Because I'm Indian, no one knows who I am or thinks I'm on any side, so they go where I tell them to.

"In the morning, I incited a riot then stepped aside when it got violent, and in the afternoon, I saved my girlfriend. I was able to get that done because I'm Indian."

John instigated things before ducking out when things got tough, but nobody placed any blame on him. You would think they should have—because of his actions, and because he showed himself to be of the same mind as the protestors—but they didn't, because of his skin color. When I went to SASCO's offices to engage them on their objectives, I was ignored; yet when I stood up to address the student community to share my views on the issue, SASCO vilified me. Black and White students were plastered with assumptions solely because of their skin color, but he was not, in this case. He played with color and got away with it because the Blacks and Whites were not making assumptions about him then.

Can "They" Be on Your Side?

With John Paul, the issue was that no one knew what to expect from an Indian person at Wits then, and that worked to his advantage in some cases. For many White people, the problem was quite the opposite: people "knew" exactly how these Whites thought and behaved. They believed they could tell all about a White person just by looking at his or her skin, and sometimes they were absolutely wrong.

One of these White people was Stephen Lowry, my history teacher at Sacred Heart, a mixed-race, private religious high school. Mr. Lowry had been born in 1961 to parents who hated apartheid, and who had seen many of their like-minded friends tossed into prison or sent into exile by the South African government. As a schoolboy, Mr. Lowry was active in the Young Christian Students, a non-racist movement dedicated to ending apartheid, where he met and befriended Black youngsters. One of his friends was a Black leader of the 1976 uprising who was imprisoned and tortured while still a teenager.

Upon completing university, where he was active in anti-apartheid protests, Mr. Lowry and his friends decided the best way for them to strike against apartheid was to refuse the compulsory military service—the South African army was, after all, used to enforce the evil system. And so, Mr. Lowry took a trip to Lesotho, then snuck back across the border. According to his passport, he was out of the country; the South African military duly received letters from him, saying he was now in England, now in Holland, traveling and studying. But he was actually in South Africa, where he wrote those letters and sent them to friends in Europe, who would apply the proper stamps and mail them to the South African draft board, thus "proving" that Mr. Lowry was not available for military service. The military wrote back saying all was fine, let us know when you return so you can "do your duty."

Mr. Lowry took a job working for the Catholic Bishops Conference, helping conscientious objectors like himself avoid military service yet stay out of jail. Through his work at the Conference, he was involved in the End Conscription Campaign (ECC), which was launched in 1984. He traveled about the country and around Europe, raising money for the ECC, and he subsequently became the organization's national treasurer. As the ECC was prohibited from raising funds outside the country, the money he gathered—plus money from others—was quietly brought into the country by the Catholic Church for the work of the ECC.

It was a dangerous time. Some of his friends and colleagues were tossed in jail. His own house was petrol-bombed, with three bombs thrown at his home. Mr. Lowry was finally snatched up by the police and detained for a couple of weeks. He didn't want to go into exile, preferring to remain in the country and teach youngsters a new way of viewing and treating both themselves and the "other." So the Church sponsored his studies and gave him the job at Sacred Heart. He was a wonderful teacher who encouraged us to be knowledgeable, read the newspapers, and to think critically about current events. This White man treated us all equally and as having great potential.

It was not only Mr. Lowry who took chances on behalf of "others"— the entire school did. Given that the South African Catholic bishops were appalled by apartheid—and had indicated at a 1976 conference that the Church could no longer comply with the apartheid laws in their school admissions—it's no wonder Sacred Heart took the risk of opening its doors in 1978 to all comers, regardless of race. Doing so was dangerous, for the government could have come down hard on the school, as well as on its individual teachers and administrators. It would have been easy for the government to harass the teachers and administrators in petty ways, doing things like making sure they received plenty of driving and parking tickets, and that their tax returns were scrupulously audited every year. As a matter of fact, as soon as Sacred Heart opened its doors to "others," the state education authorities threatened to close it down. Meetings between the Catholic school authorities and senior government officials were held to find a way of dealing with the issue. The headmaster of Sacred Heart at the time, Brother Neil McGurk, was part of the Catholic delegation made up of Archbishop George Daniel of Pretoria; Br. Jude Pieterse, chairperson of the South African Catholic Schools Association; and the senior evangelist of the Sisters of Mercy, Sr. Marion of the Dominican Sisters. Fortunately, the government backed off. Fearful of pressure from overseas that might arise were they felt to be attacking the Catholic Church, the government "only" cut back on the money it gave the school every year.

The school, led by Brother Neil McGurk, made up the lost money by raising funds elsewhere, including overseas, and by raising tuition. And it continued to defy apartheid. When the government announced a state of emergency in 1986 and sought to round up leaders of the opposition, Sacred Heart opened its doors once again, literally hiding some of these leaders at the school and at other campuses. One of these leaders, Eric Molobi, moved into a room at the school that had formerly been used as an archive. Masquerading as a chauffeur during the day, he would quietly leave the school to conduct his activities, and return just as quietly.

All went well until he was arrested by authorities in Durban. They hadn't figured out he had been hiding at Sacred College, however. Instead, they had followed an associate of his and captured Molobi when he met the associate at the Durban airport.

Another Sacred Heart campus, Sacred Heart College Primary School in Yeoville, was raided by the security police. They were after Frank Chikane, chair of the Learners Representative Council. They didn't get him because he was out of the country at the time, but someone—perhaps the security police—put some "poison powder" on his clothing that almost killed him as he was flying out of the country.

In 1986, Sacred Heart was once again caught up in violence as youth in Soweto and other areas ramped up the protests against apartheid. Once again, there was tremendous pressure to boycott school, and some Blacks who were felt to be collaborating with the authorities were murdered. One morning in June, the teachers and administrators arriving early found that someone had "necklaced" the statue of Sacred Heart that stood at the school's entrance. The statue was not set on fire, as happened when people were necklaced, but all around it were pamphlets that said:

> REMEMBER JUNE 16. On 16 June 1976 our comrades have been murdered by the present Regime!!! Our comrades got together to express their grievances against the exploitation by the racist rich capitalists, of the people. They were met by gun violence. Private schools were established for the rich and wealthy students who exploit the black people the most. JUNE 16th is a day to remember and no black students will go to school from 9th to the 30th. Students who goes to school are traitors and will be necklaced by the courts.

The presence of this pamphlet suggested it was student protestors who had necklaced the statue, but as it turned out, the state Security Forces had done so, hoping to discredit the rebellion. The same day, a junior school in Yeoville linked to Sacred Heart was bombed by the Security Forces. A state of emergency was declared a few days later. Despite these assaults, and the many other problems that arose, Sacred Heart stubbornly insisted on educating all who were interested. Not only did the school educate Blacks and other "others," the school developed a special curriculum of its own. All through the country, Black schools used special government-approved courses of study that emphasized the achievements of the Whites, downplayed or ignored those of other groups, and were geared toward turning out minimally educated Blacks qualified only for menial jobs. Sacred Heart took a different tack, for it believed that if scholars were treated as if they had potential, they would live up to that potential.

You could write an entire book about the heroic activities of Mr. Lowry, Brother Neil McGurk, and many Whites like them, as well as Sacred Heart and similar institutions. The individual stories would vary, but the main thrust would be the same: some White people and some White institutions risking life and limb in recognition of the humanity of the oppressed.

Can We Take a Blank Page Approach?

No one can ever take my Blackness away, but people can and sometimes do make assumptions about me because of my skin color. They may assume I "think like a Black person" and "act like a Black person," or that I *should* "think and act like a Black person," whatever that means to them.

People can, and sometimes do, make assumptions about Blacks, Whites, Indians, Coloureds, and members of other groups, basing these guesses—and that's all they are, guesses—on the person's skin color, accent, clothing, haircut, where they live or went to school, what book they're reading or what food they're eating, or on so many other "facts" and "reasons." But my story, along with Nic and Pauline's, and those of John Paul's, Mr. Lowry and Brother Neil McGurk's, and millions of others, proves that we really can't know a person until we get to know them.

I'm passionate about getting to know people for who they really are. When I meet them, I approach them with a nearly blank page in my mind. Over time, I fill it up with my thoughts on who they are based on my experience with them. In other words, I give them the opportunity to instruct me on how I should see them, and by implication, how I should treat them. I would like people to behave in the same way toward me, to look beyond my skin color and get to know me.

In an ideal world, there would be no labels. No one would be Black, White, or anything else, for society would be "colorless." I understand that we don't live in that kind of world and that we do, consciously or unconsciously, categorize people based on skin tone or lineage. Is it possible for us to stop there, though? Can we acknowledge that people have different skin tones and lineages without ascribing to them certain characteristics or qualities—or insisting that they lack them—just because of their skin color or lineage?

That's my dream: a world in which we see everyone else as a human being, and skin color is just a little piece of a person's outward appearance, a piece we look right past to see what is inside.

CHAPTER FIVE

FROM HATRED TO HEALING

I have every reason to hate Whites, who poisoned the world with apartheid.

Because of them, my paternal grandfather was reviled, exiled, and spent decades separated from my father and his siblings, under constant threat of kidnapping, imprisonment, and torture.

Because of them, my maternal grandfather was forced to repeatedly risk his freedom as he faced down policemen who had unjustly arrested Blacks.

Because of them, my father was murdered, shot in the head with an assault rifle. If Dad was lucky, he died instantly—but it's hard to imagine he was riding a lucky streak that day. And because of them, I lost any chance of getting to know and grow close to my dad.

My Father's Father, Bernard Gilbert Molewa

I know almost nothing about my father's father, for his anti-apartheid activities forced him to flee to neighboring Botswana before I was born. I saw him exactly twice: once when I was two years old (which hardly counts) and again at my father's funeral when I was nineteen, but that was only for a few moments.

Everything I know about Grandfather could be contained in one of those little paragraphs that appear in the newspaper obituary section: He was born in Duivelskloof in 1915, the fifth of eight children of Magdalene Selepe and Piet Molewa. He completed high school via correspondence and was a member of both the ANC and the South African Communist Party by 1943. He married Victoria Monakga, and they had four children: Richard, Thomas, Victoria, and my dad. He was arrested and detained a couple of times, and in 1964, he was again seized and tried under the Suppression of Communism Act. Facing a lengthy jail sentence, he fled to Botswana, where he was granted political asylum. (It was in Botswana that I met him for the first time.) Grandfather continued working with the ANC from afar, so the apartheid government attempted to kidnap him at least once and otherwise harassed him right up through 1990, when Nelson Mandela was released from prison. Upon returning to South Africa in 1991, after twenty-seven years in exile, Grandfather served in various posts, including representing the North West Province as a Member of Parliament from 1995 through 2004. He died on October 29, 2004, following a brief illness.

You could read that entire paragraph in less than a minute. I wish I could tell you more but apartheid kept Grandfather away from his country, his friends, and his South African family. And once Dad was gone, my connection to Grandfather was but a wisp.

The only memento I have of Grandfather is a picture I found on the Internet. It shows a thoughtful man of about fifty years. I can tell he's intelligent, a professional man, and kind, someone you could trust. There's also a sadness about him—at least, it seems to me that he is sad under the smile. During all those years of exile, did he miss speaking his native language? Or was it something more prosaic that he yearned for—perhaps visits to the old neighborhood gathering place to have a drink and listen to his favorite music? And how could he not have missed his friends and loved ones? I imagine that he thought apartheid would come to an end shortly after he was granted political asylum in Botswana. But as the years rolled by with apartheid still locked in place, did he fear that he would pass away before seeing them again? Grandfather must certainly have feared that his actions would affect my dad and his siblings. Did he ever wonder if the struggle was worth the sacrifices he made? Perhaps I'm imagining it all, or perhaps he truly was sad. I'll never know for sure.

On November 4, 2004, the South African National Assembly paid tribute to him. This record appears in the transcript of proceedings in which a member stood to propose:

That the House –

(1) *notes with sadness the untimely death of Mr. Bernard Gilbert Molewa, who passed away on the 29th of October 2004;*

(2) *recognises that Mr Molewa was a South African patriot who lived a selfless life, making an enormous contribution to the struggle for democracy in this country;*

(3) *notes that he had been detained several times under apartheid, went into exile in 1964, that he served as an ANC representative in the then German Democratic Republic, Hungary and Cuba, and also as a member of the Provincial Executive Committee of the SACP of the North West Province;*

(4) *acknowledges the dynamic contribution that Mr. Molewa made to Parliament from 1994 to 2004;*

(5) *believes that he leaves a legacy of heroism and dedicated service to the people of South Africa...*

It all sounds so very bureaucratic, but I love it. Even though I don't support his communist views, I love knowing that he mattered so much and that he accomplished so much in the struggle for a non-racial South Africa.

My Mother's Father, John Langa

I know more about my maternal grandfather because I lived with him from ages four to ten. I know that he loved music, that he played the trumpet in the Salvation Army Band as a young man, and that he was even a bandmaster at one point. He no longer had his trumpet when I knew him, but he would "play" it anyway, imitating its sound by loudly singing, "Bum, bum, bum!" He woke up singing in the morning, sang during the day, and sang with friends at get-togethers. His favorite choices were victorious songs of hope or wistful songs that opened a window to the trouble in his heart. Whether happy or longing, his songs always praised God. Although he didn't attend church regularly, he was devout in his attachment to God, believing that his earthly power flowed from his heavenly father.

There are things about Grandfather I didn't know about when I was young. Even today, the details are a bit fuzzy, for what he did for the community was not the sort of thing you would record under apartheid. It was not talked about much when I lived with Grandfather and Grandmother, so I had no idea what was going on, only that he knew a lot of people, and there was a Coloured man and his sister who came and went.

I put the pieces together after chatting with Isaac Langa, a relative of mine who was very close to my grandfather. Grandfather was vice chairman of the local soccer team, the Orlando Pirates, which gave him a lot of local prominence, even with Whites. This allowed him to develop a relationship with Mr. William Carr, the White man who ran what everyone knew as "80 Albert Street." This was the address of Johannesburg's Non-European Affairs Department, a government entity that controlled the flow of "others" in and out of the area and decided which of the "others" would be allowed to live and work in and around Johannesburg. This was a very important government department, for the city was a magnet for Black men desperate for jobs. They and their families could barely scratch out a living in the rural areas, so the men tried frantically to migrate to the cities, find work, and send money home to feed their families.

Eager to keep the Whites separated from the "others," the apartheid government had long since forcibly relocated Indians, Coloureds, and Blacks, reserving the best land and the productive cities for themselves. But they needed the "others" to work in factories in the cities and in the mines, as well as to handle other lower-level and menial jobs. So for example, if a factory in Johannesburg needed twenty new Black workers, they would send their request to 80 Albert Street, which would tally up all the requests coming in and grant the requisite number of permits to live and work in Johannesburg. These permits were vital, for a Black person caught without the proper paperwork, which was called the *dompas*, could be dragged to jail or tossed out of town.

My grandfather would go to see Mr. Carr at 80 Albert Street and "work the rules." Although he was not an attorney, he knew the regulations and could find loopholes in them. In addition, Grandfather was charismatic and charming, with a wonderful smile and a habit of greeting enemies as "my friend." So he would go to 80 Albert Street and fill out paperwork indicating he was the father or uncle of a young man who had migrated from a Bantustan to Johannesburg—or otherwise game the system to get that precious permission to work and reside in the city. He would have new arrivals live at his house, or the house of a friend, until they found work and accommodations.

Although Grandfather usually relied on charm and persuasion, he could be a warrior when necessary—indeed, he had been an enthusiastic boxer as a young man. And it was often necessary for him to march into the local police station to try to get a Black person released from custody. The police had a great deal of latitude when dealing with Blacks. They could arrest almost anyone for almost any reason, no matter how frivolous—or even fictional—it might have been. Grandfather would begin with his smile, but that was often not enough, so he would have to verbally go toe-to-toe with the policemen and their superiors, either arguing points of law he knew because he had studied the legal codes to get people released or just challenging them on the injustice of their actions.

Grandfather could have dedicated himself to getting ahead. After all, he was very smart, quite enterprising, well-connected in the Black community, and in possession of some helpful links to the White community. Against all odds, he was even able to strike a deal with BMW to own and run a BMW dealership in Soweto. There were other dealerships partially owned by Black, Coloured, or Indian people, but he was the first to have majority ownership. That's an amazing achievement, which speaks well for both parties.

On BMW's part, they had the humanity to trust a Black man with their reputation in the context of apartheid and the courage to take a financial risk. On my grandfather's part, he was amazingly successful, despite having very limited access to capital and no formal business training. He was able to purchase a petrol (gas) filling station on a large tract of land by a major street in Soweto, strike a deal with a developer to build a shopping mall there, strike another deal with BMW to build a dealership on the same land, and give himself fifty-one percent ownership in what would be the first Black majority-owned and operated BMW dealership in Johannesburg and the environs. Unfortunately, he passed away before the gas station and BMW dealership—the parts of his dream that eventually became realities—were completed.

I describe this "great-almost" not to brag about what a smart man Grandfather was, but to emphasize how much he sacrificed in the service of others. He could have used his connections and persuasive talents to set up any number of different businesses and—given his ability to work around the letter of the law—to subtly defy apartheid and earn much more money than he "should have" (that is, much more money than the authors of apartheid wanted any Black man to possess). But he didn't. Instead, he spent a great deal of his time helping others and gave a great deal of his resources to the cause.

I believe the primary reason he strove to develop the filling station/ mall/dealership was because it would offer scores of jobs to Black men and women. There, Black employees could be promoted to the technical, managerial, and other higher positions they were routinely denied. I'm sure Grandfather hoped some of them would be bold enough to leave and find their own ways forward. In other words, he was fighting for his dignity and the dignity of others. This venture would help him realize his own aspirations without requiring him to "check his dignity at the door," as did most of the jobs available to Black men and women. Neither would his employees be required to bow and scrape in hopes of holding on to a crummy job. Instead, they would be treated with respect and would rise as far as their talents might take them.

Grandfather loved people and being part of a community. He yearned to connect with others, and when he met someone who was struggling, his first thought was, *How can I help?* He had time to sit with everyone, listen to their stories, and, if he could not offer help, at least offer sympathy. Grandfather knew almost all the tribal languages and would greet everyone he met in the appropriate language if he knew what it was. If not, he loved to greet people by saying, "*Sawubona.*" It is a Zulu word which literally means "We see you." In English, the word is understood to mean "Hello," but *sawubona* recognizes the other person's humanity, not just their physical presence. For Grandfather, as for many others, saying *sawubona* was the same as saying, "I see you. How can I help you today?"

Grandfather didn't just say *sawubona*, he truly practiced it, and doing so was a part of his walking in the spirit of *ubuntu*.

My Father, Thabo Victor Molewa

I have no idea why my father died or by whose specific hand he was murdered. I do know when he died, more or less, for I was at his funeral, but seeing him laid to rest brought me no closure and no sense of being closer to him. Instead, I left the ceremony feeling ever more the outsider. I was, however, proud to discover the extent to which he had been important to the struggle against apartheid, for he was honored by the resistance movement with a 21-gun salute as his coffin, draped in the ANC flag, was lowered into the ground.

I can only sketch out my father's story, for he and my mother divorced when I was ten. Unfortunately, the split was acrimonious, and Mom made it clear that she didn't want him or his financial support. So after the divorce, I saw him fewer than a dozen times before I reestablished contact when I was eighteen years old. This was in 1992—during my first year of university—and I was in desperate need of money. Rather than risk being forced to drop out of school, I reached out to Dad. He was by this time an attorney running his own practice, and to his credit, he eagerly offered to help. Although he had remarried—and he and his wife had just welcomed a little boy into the world—he assisted me as much as he could with my on campus living expenses, and we hung out a few times. When I first saw him again after so many years, I instantly recognized his big, dark, shining brown eyes. I was surprised to discover he had a great sense of humor, a very witty tongue, and that he—unlike my mother—was eager to brag about me. Whenever we bumped into people he knew, he would introduce me as his daughter who "is in her *second year* of her Bachelor of Commerce studies at *Wits* University and is the *president* of the Commerce Students' Council at *Wits*," always emphasizing the words I've italicized. He seemed quite proud of the fact that I was president of a predominantly White male student council at a predominantly White university. I really didn't think this was as big of a deal as my dad made it out to be, but it felt great to know that he was proud of me!

Dad was born in 1951, just as apartheid was coming into full force. He studied law at Turfloop University, which was where Black Sotho-speaking people were required to study. While there, he became heavily involved in the anti-apartheid movement, joining SASO and the SRC,[9] two organizations at the forefront of the struggle at the university level. He and my mom, who was at the University of Kwa-Zulu Natal, were both involved in SASO. Through these groups he met and worked with Steve Biko, who was later murdered in jail by the authorities; Abram Tiro, who was killed by a parcel bomb believed to have been mailed by the South African security services; Ben Langa, who fell to internal violence within the resistance community; and Mamphela Ramphele, who later founded the Agang South Africa political party. Dad, with his photographic memory and wide knowledge of politics, history, and other topics, was considered to be SASO's resident expert, their "walking encyclopedia" in those days before Google.

Unfortunately, along with Tiro and other SRC members, Dad was expelled from the university in 1972 after Tiro gave a speech heavily criticizing the Bantu Education Act, which consigned Blacks to inferior education. Dad wound up working at a department store called Checkers. Although he enjoyed his job and quickly rose to department manager, he was not content to sit on the sidelines of the struggle. He managed to get back into the university in the early 1980s, rejoined the SRC, and was elected president of the student body. Upon graduating, he applied for an articled clerk position at one of South Africa's premier law firms, Cheadle, Thompson & Haysom, which had been founded in 1984 by four White men who hated apartheid: Michael Cheadle, Nicholas Haysom, Clive Thompson, and Peter Harris.

Before establishing their firm, these men had been involved in resistance-related political activities and had come to the attention of the authorities. Cheadle had been banned by the government and subjected to three years of house arrest for organizing the anti-apartheid 1973 union strikes in Durban. Haysom had been the recipient of numerous rounds of detention and solitary confinement, while Harris had had a number of runs-ins with the security police. Undeterred, the four men decided to open a law firm specializing in representing victims of apartheid as well as organizations that were fighting the nationalist apartheid government. They also deliberately recruited impressive young people of all races, making it a point to advance their careers. My dad was one of those people. He was clever and articulate, and one of the first articled clerks Cheadle, Thompson & Haysom recruited. I know this because I recently spoke to Peter Harris, hoping to learn about the man that was my father. Peter was kind enough to tell me a lot about the professional and personal sides of my father that I didn't have visibility to as a child.

Peter told me that Dad was a sharp dresser and was a social and popular guy. He was fun and easy to be with, charming, charismatic, and a genuinely nice man. Dad sailed through his articles, passed the board exam, and remained with Cheadle, Thompson & Haysom. Thanks to his iron resolve and never-wavering commitment to work, he rose quickly through the ranks to become a partner. Dedicated to the struggle, Dad spent a lot of time away from home fighting for the rights of the oppressed.

Although he had directly and indirectly suffered at the hands of the security police, he didn't have a malicious bone in his body and he remained resolutely non-racial. Peter says that Dad was a gifted mediator who was absolutely "dedicated to his clients and much loved by them."

Along with the rest of the firm, Dad was "in the trenches," representing defendants accused of subversion or treason, procuring interdicts (injunctions) to prevent the state from torturing detainees, and opposing the forced removals of Coloureds and Blacks from residential and rural areas that the apartheid government wanted to appropriate. The authorities were, as you would expect, eager to clamp down on Cheadle, Thompson & Haysom's activities, and some of the firm's lawyers found themselves in trouble with the authorities. The firm was raided once or twice by the security police, some of its lawyers were arrested, and Haysom was placed in detention for about eight months, as was another partner, Azhar Cachalia.

Dad did a fair amount of criminal work representing individuals from anti-apartheid organizations, especially in the north of the country around the Turfloop area. This required him to be away from home in remote areas for weeks at a time while running trials. Together with Haysom, Dad represented the late Peter Mokaba, who was the head of the ANC Youth League, and worked (at least in the early stages) with Haysom on the Delmas Four treason trial. During Dad's work on some of these trials, he and Peter sometimes traveled outside of the country to meet with exiled leaders, such as Mzwai Piliso, then head of the ANC's Security Department; Chris Hani, who was Chief of Staff of Umkhonto we Sizwe; Penuell Maduna, then Deputy Head of the ANC Legal Department; and Ronnie Kasrils, who headed up the ANC Military Intelligence. On one of these trips to Zambia, Dad even managed to meet up with my exiled grandfather at the Pamodzi Hotel!

Dad also worked quite extensively on employment law cases. Since these labor law issues are often handled in mediation, Dad decided to take a mediation course. He took to it instantly and soon became highly sought after, especially in the employment and political arenas. I wish

I knew how and why he became one of the top mediators in the country. It may have helped that he was one of the few Black mediators, but there must have been something more. Maybe it was because he was well-spoken and had a great memory, which would allow him to recall the relevant law at just the right moment. Perhaps it was the fact that he was so likeable; maybe he could truly be sympathetic to both sides, listening to their stories with an open heart and then gently bringing them to an agreement.

What I learned about the nature of his work-related activities surprised me. When I was growing up, all I knew was that he represented workers and trade unions on employment law matters. I certainly understood that union activity in South Africa was, by definition, a political matter. The fact that "others" unionized was a challenge to the White-run corporations that profited greatly on the backs of the "others," who had little choice but to accept miserable working conditions and pay. Adding to the tension was the fact that many trade unions organized themselves under the banner of the Congress of South African Trade Unions, which allied itself with the ANC and South African Communist Party. This made unions even more dangerous in the eyes of the government. So I understood that there was a political element to the work he did, but I hadn't realized that it went so far beyond employment-law-related matters.

Luthule House, the ANC headquarters, has not been able to provide me with any information on whether Dad was a member of the ANC, for the records from those distant years are not readily available. He was certainly linked to the organization, which continually challenged the apartheid regime via "stay-aways," peaceful protests, mobilization of the international community to pressure the South African government, and other means, including sabotage, bombings, and armed attacks on police stations. The government responded with violence of its own, imprisoning, torturing, and assassinating members of the rebellion. As far as I know, Dad did not carry a gun. But he was aligned with a forbidden, sometimes-violent resistance movement, and as an attorney, he could do some damage to the regime.

We didn't speak about Dad's ANC activities when I reestablished contact with him in the early 1990s because we only met a few times and were more focused on getting to know each other. And even if we had had more time, I doubt he would have told me everything he was doing. Remember, these were dangerous times. Yes, Nelson Mandela had been released from prison, and White voters had, through a nationwide referendum, decided to move away from apartheid, but the nation's future was as frightening as it was unknown. Various political factions fought for the right to shape the government-to-be, and certain members of the government security forces fanned the flames, for they did not want to see the establishment of a dispensation in which the government reflected the wishes of the majority.

Even as Mandela was calling for peace and reconciliation, violence between the dominant ANC party and the Inkatha Freedom Party (IFP)—then led by Mangosuthu Buthelezi, who was considered an apartheid-system collaborator—flared to frightening levels. The fact that covert government security forces were supplying the IFP with large quantities of weapons didn't help matters.

It was against this bloody backdrop that the National Peace Accord (NPA) structures were established, and representatives of the government and various parties met to find ways to prevent future violence. These included bringing people together at the local level to mediate disputes. My father played a role in this, heading up an NPA region covering Johannesburg, East Rand, West Rand, and other areas. While I can't fully flesh out the details of my father's work with the Accord, I can tell you that with several thousand political deaths being recorded yearly, inserting yourself between warring parties was not the safest thing to do.

For example, Thokoza, where my father spent a lot of time working, was home to a hostel the IFP used as a fortress from which to launch attacks against the community. In one of these attacks, entire blocks of houses were burned and destroyed, and fierce street battles raged between the self-defense units of the ANC and the IFP. The situation was so bad that a joint operations center—staffed by representatives from all political parties, the South African Police Services, members of the Wits/ Vaal Peace Secretariat, and observers from the United Nations, British Commonwealth, and African Union—was set up within the grounds of the Natalspruit Hospital in Thokoza. My dad spent a lot of time in that joint operations center, assisting and directing operations as well as mediating and giving advice to the various parties.

Other forms of violence—assassinations, bombings, disappearances, and abductions by the security forces—spurred the resistance organizations to create an Independent Board of Inquiry into Informal Repression, which counted among its leaders Peter Harris, Bishop Desmond Tutu, and Frank Chikane. Dad assisted the board in investigating these terrible matters.

By this time, Dad had left Cheadle, Thompson & Haysom and had started his own firm, which focused on union cases and mediation. It was while Dad was traveling to oversee a civic meeting in Thokoza that he was murdered. No one knows by whose particular hand he was slain or why. But we do know that 1993, the year Dad died, was not a good one for the ANC. Besides my father, Chris Hani was assassinated right outside his house and many other struggle stalwarts fell.

I learned of Dad's death while on summer break from Wits, when a relative called my mom, who passed the news on to me. I don't recall either of us saying much at the time; I think we were just in shock. I had rung his house just a week or so earlier but was not told that he had gone missing. Discovering that he was not only dead but had been missing for a while made it all much worse in my mind.

I was in denial for several days, hoping to hear that he was really still alive. That's how I felt, as if he was still with me. Finally, reality broke through my denial, and I couldn't hold my grief back. I shut myself up in my bedroom, prayed that he would rise up from the dead, screamed and shouted, and bawled my eyes out. I don't remember which words I used, only that I felt a deep sense of pain, loss, and a desire to see him again in person. I was so mad at having lost him. I prayed and screamed and cried for what felt like hours, and when it was all over, I felt calm and at peace. Healed even. I never cried again over losing him, not even at his funeral.

I really felt like an outsider at my dad's funeral. Listening to the speeches, I felt sad about how I was cut out of his life. I was not invited to sit with the family and was not even listed as his child in his obituary. It was as if I had never existed. I do remember thinking that it was weirdly reflective of how our relationship had been from the time my mom and he divorced until about a year before his death. Thankfully, when it was time for family members to throw sand in the grave pit, someone tapped me on the shoulder and instructed me to move closer to the grave pit and throw sand in. I have no idea who that person was, but I am grateful to her, for the small act of adding a little sand to his final resting place was very cathartic for me. I felt that it publicly affirmed my connection to him.

I attended Dad's funeral when I was nineteen years old. Now, over twenty years later, the only mementos I have of him are a brief report that appeared in the documents of the South African Truth Commission, which was established after the fall of apartheid to, among other things, document the damage done to the nation and this note in the Independent Board of Inquiry's Report for December 1993 and January 1994:[10]

6.9 Thabo Molewa

Lawyer and mediator, Thabo Molewa was murdered on his way to adjudicate elections at a civic meeting in Thokoza. Molewa did not arrive at the meeting on December 11. Despite his disappearance on the 11th, his body was only identified at the Germiston mortuary on December 24. According to the mortuary records, Molewa's body was found two hours after he had left his home in Spruitview. His body was found in Mngadi section Katlehong. According to the SAP he had been shot in the head with an AK 47. Molewa's car has not been recovered although his bank cards and other personal items were found in a stretch of field not far from his home.

The police have announced a R50 000 award for any information that will lead to the arrest and prosecution of the perpetrators.

Was Dad killed for something he did or something he knew? Had he uncovered information that would hugely embarrass someone or some party, so they decided to silence him? Was someone settling an old grudge before the turnover of power?

I've wondered, but it doesn't really matter, as I have forgiven and moved on. I have forgiven those who created the conditions for his death, those directly responsible for his death, and those who chose not to acknowledge me at his funeral, though fully aware of my connection to him. All that matters now is that I never got to know him, who he really was, and how he became such a highly sought-after mediator. I never got to build the relationship of love and trust every daughter wishes to have with her father. And he never had the father's joy of seeing his little girl—now a young woman—fly from the nest, wobble a bit as she learns to navigate the world, then soar. He never saw me become an attorney and we never got to swap stories about law school, our careers, or his adventures in court, mediation sessions, and with clients. He never met his grandchildren whom I birthed, and he never saw his nation become free. He never knew how much he had succeeded in so many ways. He lost so much, as did I, for I lost him.

An Invitation to Hatred

In 2003, I lived in London for a couple of months. This was during a time when I was with Deutsche Bank's global markets team in Johannesburg and I was assigned to London for training. One day while walking home after work, I stopped at a traffic light. While waiting for the light to change, I happened to catch the eye of a pleasant-looking middle-aged man with dark hair and a long beard, dressed in a long, flowing white robe. I don't know what this clothing symbolized, but he looked quite regal. After a brief exchange of greetings, during which he learned I was from Johannesburg, he launched into a diatribe against White people. All of them. He said this, and I'm paraphrasing because the words spilled out of him so fast and with too much hatred for me to take them all in: "You are a Black woman from South Africa, so you know Whites are full of hatred and evil—every single one of them! In most places in the world where there is discord, Whites are at the bottom of it. Without Whites, there would be no hatred, no divisions, no evil." He went on and on, apparently believing that since I was a Black woman from South Africa, I would naturally agree with him.

He was not the only person to make this type of assumption. Sometime later, I had an exchange with a colleague in Boston, a White male who was trying to figure out how I could be from South Africa and not be angry toward White people.

I opened this chapter by saying that I have every reason to hate Whites, who slathered the infection of discrimination and apartheid over us. That's true. But to do so would deny them of their humanity. It would deny me of mine as well, for when I consciously and deliberately tell myself that an entire race of human beings is irredeemably vile, lacking even a shred of that which makes us human, I have lost my way. I have broken my connection with that which makes me human. And when I consciously and deliberately see "them"—whoever "them" might be—as less than human, I am giving license to everyone else who wishes to see the "other" in the same way as the Nazis saw the Jews, as the Hutu saw the Tutsi, as the Japanese saw the Chinese during World War II, and as so many groups have seen the "others" so many times since humans began recording their history.

It is natural to become angry with those who have done you harm. It is natural to want to strike back, even to go beyond justice and take revenge. And it is just as natural to engage with those who have hurt you and to share your grievances in ways that build bridges rather than destroy them, to forgive those who have wronged you, to bind wounds, and to seek to walk together as brothers—to practice *ubuntu*, as I learned from my mother's father John Langa, whom I lived with during my childhood.

No Man Is an Island

The African approach to life known as *ubuntu* finds its expression in many tribal languages. A Sotho phrase captures the concept well: "Motho ke motho ka batho," which translates to, "I am who I am because of others." In other words, life is about more than just me. It's about us, about community and interdependence, and about realizing that unless other people are whole, I am not and cannot be whole.

Why is this so? Why can't I just take care of myself and my family while not harming others? Shouldn't that be enough?

It might be, if we were all completely separate from each other, living in our own little spheres. So long as one sphere didn't smash into another sphere, everything would be fine. But that's not how life is; we're not in our own little spheres. Instead, life is a series of relationships between you and your loved ones; you and your larger family; you and your neighbors; you and the people at work; you and the folks in your neighborhood, city, and country; you and the fellow members of your faith; you and those of the many other faiths; you and the people of your "race" and of all other "races"; and on and on. We are all in so many relationships—of differing intensities, with different obligations to each other and different histories of good and bad experiences—that it is impossible to plot it all out.

This much is clear: we are all linked to everyone else in one way or another. Everything we do affects everyone else to one degree or another, and everything others do affects us. That is why we cannot be whole unless everyone is whole. We all live in the same giant sphere, inhale the collective love and the collective hate, and enjoy the collective acceptance whilst being stung by the collective bitterness. Just as fallout from a nuclear weapon detonated anywhere on Earth eventually reaches every part of the planet, just as new diseases leap over national boundaries to spread everywhere, so do hatred, resentment, racism, and all the other harmful "isms" eventually poison the entire planet along with everyone on it.

That is why new hatred is never the answer to past hatred, new racism is never the cure for past racism, and new economic oppression is never the solution to past economic oppression. New hatred, racism, and economic oppression are just as poisonous as the old ones, and as long as that poison is allowed to exist, it will spread. You will surely be tainted by it, or even become the evil you once sought to eliminate.

Ubuntu is my preferred solution to resolving the upset remaining from past ills, for it encourages us to realize that we are all imperfect human beings struggling with our fears and doubts, sometimes allowing our pettiness or cruelty to spew onto others. I may not, for example, have been racist during the apartheid era, but I had other flaws. Perhaps I treated others as less than because of their religion, nationality, body type, accent, educational level, lack of athletic prowess, or looks. Being non-racist is good, but if, instead, I think I'm intellectually superior or better looking than others, does that make me a good person? Does it give me the right to say I'm better than the one who looks down on others because of skin color or any other reason?

Apartheid was an abomination, and it's perfectly natural to respond to it with anger or bitterness. But when we cling to bitterness—or we (consciously or unconsciously) repress it instead of releasing it and forgiving—we're elevating the way in which others have hurt us above the way in which we may have hurt others. We become blind to the need to seek forgiveness from others for our wrongdoings, no matter what they may be. We are in effect saying that their wrongful acts toward us are more impactful than our wrongful acts toward others. We are overlooking the fact that those who harmed us have a blind spot or weakness, just as we do, which is manifested in a different way. Instead, we see others as being the weakness and the misguided action, and we sweep aside all the other things that they are. In other words, we no longer see them as being human, with the same weaknesses from which we suffer. We strip away their humanity as completely as they once stripped away ours, and we become like two warriors in the arena, competing to see who will be first to slay the other.

Don't get me wrong. I'm not calling for turning a blind eye to bigoted behavior. But I am asking that we work on removing the "logs" from our own eyes, even as we encourage others to remove the "specks" from theirs. I'm also asking that we keep in mind that if we believe that we are capable of growing and of opening up more of ourselves to others as we do so, we should be open to believing that it is equally possible for others to get to that point, too.

When the man on the London street corner went off on a diatribe against Whites, I listened for a while before replying, "I don't know that we can say that evil is intrinsic to White people. I believe everyone has the capacity for evil as well as the capacity for good. It's about which direction we choose to go. Some of us choose to give in to evil impulses, and some of us strive to seek goodness. Those who choose to be evil must be resisted. And I don't believe that blaming all the world's problems on a race of people solely because of their skin color is right."

Then we noticed that the light had changed, and we went our separate ways.

Shouldering the Burden

There's an African expression in the Xhosa language: "Izandla ziyahlambana." It literally means, "The hands wash each other." Figuratively, it means that we help each other, and it can even be understood as this: "As I shoulder your burden today, you'll shoulder mine another day." This is a perfect expression of *ubuntu*, for it reminds us that we all do best when we recognize that every person is valuable and we take care of each other. This is also a key lesson I learned from John Langa, who shouldered the burdens of countless people by opening his tiny house to everyone, offering them advice, helping them find a place to live or work, going to 80 Albert Street to negotiate with the apartheid authorities on their behalf, and even going into the police station to try to rescue those who had been unjustly imprisoned. My grandfather had time to listen to everyone, no matter how "unimportant" they may have been.

South Africa no longer practices apartheid, and Jim Crow has disappeared from the United States, where I now live, but I am delighted to find that there are many ways to carry on the *ubuntu* I learned from John Langa. On a few occasions, I have invited friends who were in transition or facing financial challenges to move in with me, either on their own or along with their children. Some have stayed for weeks and others months, yet my guest-filled house never feels crowded, for I remember hearing of how my grandparents would open their house to people in need of assistance. I also remember having to wee in a bucket at night when I was young rather than make the scary trip to the outside toilet in the dark, so seeing guests' toothbrushes on my bathroom counter gives me the pleasure of knowing they are safe and comfortable while they look for a new job and a place to live.

As I open my house to others, take the time to listen to others, and offer whatever assistance I can to them, I think of John Langa. I also think of my father who, although he battled the apartheid government, found a special pleasure in bringing people together through mediation. And I think of his father who fought for decades to help restore freedom and dignity to Indians, Coloureds, Blacks, and all others oppressed by apartheid. I am thankful that I live in a much better world than they did, thanks to them and too many others to name. And I am thankful that I still have the opportunity to practice *ubuntu*, to see others—all others—as human beings who are made in the image of God, and to respond to them with an open heart. Each time I take a moment to really "see" others or help them, I feel I have helped the world heal, just a little bit.

In his poem "No Man Is an Island," English poet John Donne wrote, "Any man's death diminishes me, / Because I am involved in mankind." I like to flip that around and say, "Everybody's growth and pleasure enhance me because I am involved in mankind."

CHAPTER SIX

WHERE ARE YOU LOOKING?

As I sit down to write this chapter, I'm wondering what to say, what my "where-to-from-here?" message actually is. In truth, I know precisely what it is, but a part of me is holding back because it's not a popular, feel-good message. But I believe it's important to address it, and so I will, letting the verbal brickbats fly as they may.

As a Black woman born to and raised in apartheid-era Soweto, whose ancestors suffered and rebelled as much as anyone else, I know that we Blacks have suffered greatly and that we are, to some degree, still dealing with the aftereffects of the past, whether we live in South Africa, in the United States, or in other countries where we have historically been suppressed or persecuted. But I feel we miss the mark when we too readily succumb to the temptation to allow the evils and hurts we endured in the past—or that we may continue to endure—to lead us into supporting political parties without regard to their ability to lead us into a bright and prosperous future; to seeing ourselves as victims, as we sometimes do; and to ascribing the evils of the past to all White people, continually beating them over the head with the club of "White privilege."

There's no doubt that the evils perpetrated against us were wrong and that they produced inequalities that will take some time—perhaps many years—to address, but I wonder if dwelling on the evils and hurts engendered by racism helps. After all, clinging to this cannot undo what happened. I wonder if this isn't a trap that serves to misdirect our energies, binding us so firmly to anger and indignation that it paralyzes us and prevents us from moving forward to create better lives for ourselves and our posterity.

Looking to and Preparing for the Future

Let me step back a bit and pull together some of the strands of my life story, going all the way back to my great-grandmother Khokho. Apartheid and family conditions meant that Khokho spent her work life cleaning the houses of Whites. But she aspired to more for her two daughters and set in motion a multigenerational arc that led to my being among the first wave of "others" to move into formerly predominantly White professional firms.

Working for a well-off, White, Jewish family, Khokho noticed that books were important, as was being self-disciplined. There wasn't much she could do with this observation but she could, and did, imagine a better life for her daughters. So she pushed them to be disciplined and to excel in their studies. My grandmother, whom I called Mamkhulu did so, and she qualified to be a nurse. Family considerations later led her to switch from nursing to clerking, and apartheid ensured that she would never rise a single step on the work ladder, even though she was such a good clerk that her White bosses occasionally sent her from store to store to handle problems in her field.

Mamkhulu, in turn, pushed her daughter—my mother Esther—to study hard. And once again, apartheid stood in the way. While attending university, Mom joined protests against apartheid and ended up dropping out of school. Many years would pass before she returned to university and qualified as an attorney.

Still, the dream that there might be something better remained strong. Both Mom and Mamkhulu sacrificed so that I might attend a private Black school that offered a better education than did the Black public schools, and later, I was able to attend mixed-race, private junior high and high schools that taught students of all colors in defiance of apartheid. The dream finally paid off, for apartheid fell as I was in university; afterward, I was among the first group of "others" who pushed their way into firms that had formerly been predominantly White.

The point I want to make with this brief review of family history is that what you believe—what you dream of for yourself and for your children—is very powerful. Three generations of women—Khokho, Mamkhulu, and Mom—were continually slapped around by apartheid. My female forebears could have focused on the bad in their lives, of which there was plenty. They could have crafted a victim narrative, but instead they looked to the future. They were willing to do whatever it took, continuing to push for three generations to see their dream come true. Their long-denied-but-never-abandoned dream was based on the idea that being educated and self-disciplined will get you ahead in life.

That was the first of three lessons that shaped my approach to life. Actually, it was two lessons in one: the value of focusing on something powerfully positive, and the value of education and self-discipline. In other words, believe that the future has possibilities, and prepare yourself to embrace them.

Risking It All Yet Still Embracing Ubuntu

I know more about my female forebears than I do about my forefathers, for due to a bitter divorce, my father Victor Thabo Molewa was mostly absent from my life between the time I was ten and eighteen, and I had only a brief opportunity to reconnect with and get to know him better before he was slain. As for his father—my grandfather—I met him just twice, once when I was two years old and again at my father's funeral when I was nineteen. Nevertheless, I did learn an important lesson from them, as well as from my maternal grandfather John Langa: stand up for what you believe is right, even if taking the stand may place you in danger.

My paternal grandfather Bernard Molewa began rebelling against oppressive restrictions set in place by the Whites even before apartheid was locked in place by law in the early 1950s. While still in his early thirties, he was an active member of the ANC as well as the South African Communist Party, which also fought apartheid. Before his children were grown, Grandfather was forced to flee the country and spent twenty-seven years in political exile in Botswana, Cuba, and East Germany as he continued his work with the ANC and South African Communist Party. Upon returning to South Africa in the early 1990s, he served in parliament until he died in 2004.

While Grandfather risked his life standing up for what is right, my father literally gave his life for the same cause. He allied himself with the resistance movement in university and was expelled for his anti-apartheid activities. When he finally got back into university and earned his law degree, he immediately went to work for a law firm that was unabashedly anti-apartheid and that challenged the government over and over again, to the point where attorneys from the firm were harassed and imprisoned by the then-government.

But even as Dad was confronting apartheid head on, he devoted much of his efforts to mediation and to helping people overcome their anger and their urge to bash each other—in favor, instead, of reaching agreement and coming back together. In so doing, he became one of the country's top mediators. Unfortunately, he was slain, shot in the head with an AK-47 while traveling to adjudicate elections.

In many ways, Dad was like John Langa, my maternal grandfather. Although not an attorney, John Langa regularly went to bat for oppressed Black people by mastering the apartheid regulations that determined where Blacks were allowed to live and work, and then poking his fingers through every loophole he could find, in order to help Black men live in Soweto, put them near jobs, and then help find those jobs. The pay and working conditions were often miserable, but at least it was a job, and to a Black man under apartheid, that was precious. John Langa also went toe-to-toe with the police, boldly striding into their stations to argue on behalf of many Blacks who had been arrested for reasons Whites would not have been. It was dangerous, but he was determined and fearless.

He was also determined that I would be educated well and prepared for a better future. It was he who suggested that I transfer to a mixed-race private school, where I would receive a better education and learn to interact with people of all races, and he kept pushing my mom to find a way to make that happen.

Like my father, John Langa declined to hate the Whites who oppressed him and his "kind." Instead, both men sought to heal wounds, one through mediation and the other through engaging in the spirit of *sawubona*, which recognizes the other person's humanity—no matter what their skin color or affiliation may be—and is thus a part of practicing *ubuntu*. This was the second lesson that shaped my approach to life. The third lesson came from my mother Esther Langa.

Choosing to Make Your Choices

Unlike most African mothers, my mom took a *laissez faire* approach to raising me. Rather than placing severe restrictions on my actions and punishing me every time I misbehaved, she continually pushed me to understand that every single thing I do and every single choice I make have consequences. She taught me to think these consequences through very carefully and to take responsibility for avoiding unwanted consequences.

That by itself is a powerful lesson, but there was more—as I discovered when I called her from school one day, asking her to bring the bag containing my gym clothes, which I had forgotten to take with me that morning. I was shocked when she said no, but I realized she was teaching me to take responsibility for making the right choices. It's not enough to avoid making the wrong choices; it is equally important that you work toward your goals and take personal responsibility for turning your dreams into reality by being where you need to be, bringing what you need to bring, learning what you need to learn, and so on. To do this, of course, you must have a dream. You must believe that there is something worth working toward, even if it takes three generations or more to get there.

Choosing to avoid trouble is a vital first step. Choosing to do what it takes to turn a dream into reality is the next. It's a big step, and it's a difficult one, for it requires that we stop reflexively pointing the finger of blame at others, regardless of whether that is warranted or not, and turn it instead toward ourselves. It demands that we take responsibility for our lives, for our failures as well as our successes. Yes, external factors always exist, and they can press down heavily on our shoulders, but it is still (and always will be) up to us to choose to move forward or not.

Khokho made that choice decades ago when the way forward never amounted to more than an inch or two for a Black person in South Africa. My father made the same choice and paid for it with his life. Today, with apartheid consigned to the ash heap of history, the road ahead is wide open. Your journey may be bumpy, and you may be starting farther back on the road than others, but it is now your journey to make; the choices you make will largely determine what that journey will be.

What Choices Are Being Made Today?

South Africa has made many empowering choices, demonstrating its belief in the future, including creating a Truth and Reconciliation Commission to help the nation uncover and forgive past sins. The Rainbow Nation, though, is still very young, so we cannot yet say whether it will be enriched over the long run by the desire to create a future in which all citizens can proudly say they are members of an inclusive, prosperous, and generous society—or whether the nation will sink into a morass of greed, corruption, retribution, and fear, spurred by the desire for "my group" to reign supreme.

When considering how South Africa's future may be shaped, it may be helpful to look to the example of Black Americans whose community I became part of when I became a United States citizen.[11] Although Black

Americans were technically freed from slavery in the mid-1800s, Black Americans only began emerging from the nation's cruel and restrictive Jim Crow laws in the 1960s. Although the comparison is inexact, if for no other reason than that Blacks are overwhelmingly in the majority in South Africa while Blacks in America are a minority, we can still draw some parallels.

Some fifty-odd years later, the United States is still working through the aftereffects of its racist past, including wealth and income inequality; a paucity of major corporations headed by Blacks; a lack of diversity in a number of neighborhoods, stemming from prior "redlining" regulations; large-scale incarceration of Black men; and concerns that some police officers treat Blacks differently than Whites. Some Black Americans blame "White America" for these issues.

It is certainly true that White Americans, on average, have more money and wealth than Black Americans. A study conducted by the Center for Global Policy Solutions and the Research Network on Racial and Ethnic Inequality at Duke University revealed that for every dollar held by White American households, Black households have just six cents. The Institute for Policy Studies and the Corporation for Economic Development also conducted research into this and concluded that it would take 228 years for the average Black American household to attain the same level of wealth held by the average White American household today. As if that were not bleak enough, a study conducted by Prosperity Now (formerly CFED) and the Institute for Policy Studies concluded that by 2053, Black households will have a median wealth of zero! These statistics on wealth are alarming, and unfortunately, income-focused statistics offer no comfort. According to the US Census Bureau, the real median income for Whites in 2015 was $62,950, compared to only $36,898 for Blacks.

These are just a few of the many studies looking at the huge gaps in various measures of prosperity among different groups, and they raise the question, "Why?" Why are Black Americans still so far behind? It's generally accepted that these disparities stem from more than two hundred years of slavery; more than a century's worth of discrimination in housing, employment, voting laws, and other practices following the end of slavery; and federal policies benefiting those who already possess wealth and opportunity as opposed to those who do not, and the fact that as accumulated wealth is transferred from generation to generation, those who do not have are more likely to be caught up in poverty cycles that are as vicious as they are hard to break.

Given the centuries of slavery and discrimination that Black Americans have been forced to endure, it's no wonder that disparities exist. And it's no surprise that White Americans are so far ahead in measures of wealth and income. But interestingly enough, as I continued looking into this, I learned that Whites are not at the top of the income ladder—Asians are. The median annual household income for Asian Americans—$77,166— is higher than that of White Americans. As for wealth, Asian Americans are on their way to surpassing White Americans as the wealthiest group in the United States.[12] This is despite the fact that Asians were severely discriminated against when they began arriving in the United States during the 1800s. They were subjected to often severe, racially based codes and covenants. Chinese immigrants were massacred in race riots in the late 1800s, and more than one hundred thousand Japanese Americans were rounded up and held in internment camps during World War II. Granted, Asians were never enslaved but there is a strong history of discrimination against Asian Americans. They are quickly bridging the White-Asian wealth gap, however, and they are now at the top of the income ladder.

Though some believe otherwise, many experts agree that education has played—and continues to play—a key role in this rapid and continuing advance, and Asian Americans have, as a group, chosen to make education a major priority.

Which Paths to Moving Forward?

What choices will we, as a community, make going forward? How do we see our future, and what do we think will bring us closer to our goals?

Do we believe that pursuing an education, exercising self-discipline, and making good lifestyle choices will make a difference?

I believe we should, for the choices we make now will determine how our community fares in the future. Education, for example, largely correlates with income later in life. Specifically, high school graduates earn $8,000 more per year than non-graduates on average, while those with bachelor degrees earn $22,000 more than high school graduates. The difference between those with advanced degrees and high school dropouts is stark: $66,857 versus $20,361. Statistics show that Blacks are moderately more likely than Whites—and significantly more likely than Asians—to drop out of high school. A similar disparity exists at the college level, with seventy-five percent of Asian Americans enrolled in or completing college, as compared to fifty-two percent of Whites and thirty-nine percent of Blacks. This educational hierarchy matches perfectly with the breakdown of annual family income: Asian Americans on the top, Whites in the middle, and Blacks at the bottom.

A 2015 *US News and World Report*[13] article noted that "only 18 percent of African-American fourth-graders were proficient in reading and only 19 percent scored as proficient in math... The eighth-grade numbers were even worse, with only 16 percent of African-American students proficient in reading and 13 percent proficient in math."

When Blacks were held as slaves in the United States, Blacks were denied an education. In fact, it was illegal for slaves to read, write, and do math in most slave states. Today, we are no longer faced with these restrictions. Isn't it tragic that now that we have the right and opportunity to learn how to read and master many subjects, we're (collectively speaking) not grabbing on to it with both hands? What would those of our ancestors who could not read say? Or those who fought and suffered to end the "separate but equal" system that was anything but equal? Why aren't we vigorously challenging those who say that speaking well and being educated are "acting white"? If not for our sake, then for our children's sake? Why aren't we continually encouraging each other to "learn, baby, learn, so that we can earn, baby, earn," as Dr. Martin Luther King Jr. once implored us to?

What of the "Family Path" as a Way Forward?

In addition to enjoying high levels of wealth and education, Asian Americans are more likely than other groups to be raised in stable, two-parent families: only sixteen percent are born to single-parent households.

A two-parent household is important, for statistics show that children of single-parent households are more likely to drop out of high school and to be neither in school nor working. Those from single-parent households who are in school have, on average, poorer attendance records and lower grade point averages than their peers who live with both parents. Children of single-parent households are less likely to go to college and more likely to become teen mothers. According to the National Center for Juvenile Justice, seventy percent of youths in the criminal justice system come from single-parent households, and the poverty rate for children in single-parent families is 35.2 percent compared to 8.2 percent among children from married-couple families. Yet seventy percent of Black American children are born to and raised in single-parent households, usually ones headed by a woman. Might not our community be strengthened if we were to emphasize the importance of family, with two parents providing love, guidance, and financial support to our children?

I understand that we can't plan everything in life, and plans often go awry. But we can make a deliberate effort to ensure that we are prepared to be parents before actually becoming parents. And should the family split, as happened to mine through divorce (twice!), we can ask ourselves whether it is better for the parents to deal with their anger toward each other or let the venom fly. When my parents divorced, my mother told my father to take a hike. As a result, I was without a father's love and support for many years. Having been through this experience, I could easily have replicated my past when my marriage to Matt ended. Matt could also have sought to walk away from his kids or to deny me access to them. But I chose not to replicate my past. And Mom, having learned from her mistake, encouraged me not to. Similarly, because Matt loves our children and is a very dedicated parent, he very much wanted to continue to be in their lives and also wanted me to continue to have access to our kids, and so with hard work, we were able to make the necessary emotional adjustments and continue to work together to raise our children. It wasn't easy at first, but we are now good friends who are supportive of each other, and the results are well worth it.

In the United States, Asian Americans make up 5.3 percent of the population but only 1.3 percent of the prison population.[14] Black Americans, on the other hand, constitute a large percentage of the prison population, way out of proportion to our numbers in the general population, and we are equally overrepresented amongst those prisoners who have committed violent crimes. Some of this—too much of this—is related to discriminatory attitudes embedded in the justice system and poverty. Much of it, however, is related to a lack of fathers living with their partners and children, to gangs, to the widespread feeling that there's no point in staying in school, and to other factors over which we, the Black community, have control.

What of Our Friends?

One thing we certainly have control of is our circle of friends and acquaintances, those people with whom we associate and to whom we expose our children. Are we spending time with people who encourage us to achieve more? Or are we keeping company with those who may lure us into a lifestyle characterized by mediocrity, drugs, gangsterism, and crime? And if we are keeping company with unsavory characters, are we considering how this may influence our offsprings' attitudes toward education, work, crime, and other issues?

What of Our Bootstraps?

The Black community in the United States is economically weak, as can be seen, for example, by comparing the abysmally low levels of Black wealth and business ownership to those of Whites and other groups.

There is absolutely no doubt that the Black community was economically hamstrung by slavery, Jim Crow, and racism. There's also no doubt that some degree of racism continues to this day—which may, from time to time, impede economic progress. But as some Americans, including Star Parker, author of *Uncle Sam's Plantation*, have pointed out—there is another, seriously debilitating factor at play today, and that is the generational cycles of dependence created by the large-scale state welfare initiated by President Lyndon Johnson in the mid-1960s with his "war on poverty." Despite the more than fifteen *trillion* dollars spent since then, the rate of Black poverty remains the same, and remains twice as high as that of the nation as a whole.

Welfare is a reasonable approach to helping people get over the bumps in life and taking care of those who are unable to care for themselves. But when it becomes all-embracing, when the government allows people to believe that they need not expend any effort to secure housing, food, and so much more, it is dangerous. Making people reliant on the state robs them of initiative and the ability to stand on their own two feet, a vital skill that is like a muscle which withers away if not exercised regularly. The phrase "pulling yourself up by your own bootstraps" may sound like a hackneyed cliché, but think about what happens when you keep pulling on those bootstraps over the course of a lifetime. Your hands become stronger, as do your arms and back. Your mind begins to think of better ways to accomplish the task. You become prouder and more willing to trust in yourself as you move from success to success, and more determined to behave in ways that will protect what you have already accomplished.

That's not to say that we should never assist people. I certainly benefited from a scholarship provided by BMW that allowed me to complete my studies at Sacred Heart College, a private school that defied apartheid by embracing students of all stripes. These funds were tremendously helpful, but they were provided for a specific purpose (tuition costs only), and period of time, and were contingent on certain academic requirements being met. The scholarship gave me a leg up, but it was up to me to continue tugging on my bootstraps once I graduated.

I was able to do so because I learned a powerful lesson from my mom, grandmother, and great-grandmother, who insisted on taking care of themselves and their families to the best of their ability, rather than depending on hand-outs. They did so knowing that working couldn't possibly make them wealthy and, in some cases, was only marginally more remunerative than not working. They worked hard because they knew that working and striving and believing in yourself, that occasionally failing and even being slapped down, is important for your sense of self-worth. It strengthens you in the long run and strengthens your resolve and ability to climb that next hill—and the next, and the next.

Climbing Forward

With Black Americans being more likely to drop out of high school and college, and more likely to be raised in single-parent households, is it any wonder we continue to struggle to break out of the cycle of poverty engendered by slavery and Jim Crow and to have less income and wealth?

I'm not saying that any remaining vestiges of discrimination will vanish once these few issues are remedied. But I am insisting that we begin by looking to ourselves. I'm insisting that we embrace education, emphasize the importance of both parents being involved in raising and guiding children, encourage the avoidance of teen pregnancy and criminal life, and make good lifestyle choices. Yes, I am well aware of the fact that generational cycles of poverty and other deep-seated problems make it more difficult for our community to address these issues. But unless we do—unless we develop a positive vision of the future and work hard to make it reality—we will continue to earn less than other groups, serve more time in jail, and have children we are ill-prepared to care for.

I am also very aware of the fact that even as one obstacle is overcome, another one appears, and there are often two, five, or fifty more obstacles after that. This can be horribly frustrating, but as Nelson Mandela once noted, no matter how many more hills you need to climb after ascending one, the best thing to do is start climbing. So, yes, it may be true that as a Black person with a bachelor's degree, you may earn more income yet still have to work harder to amass wealth than would a White person who dropped out of school. Don't let that hold you back from pursuing an education. You may find yourself in a work situation where literally all your non-Black peers, including those who joined the company after you did, are being promoted while you remain stuck, for no apparent good reason. I know how this feels, for it has happened to me. More than once, I have been expected to accomplish just as much, if not more than others, despite being allotted lesser resources. More than once, I have been expected to be twice as good as my peers in order to rise to the next level, while a single misstep defined my entire work output—the same kind of misstep that was generally overlooked when committed by others. And more than once, leadership has stood by silently as this has happened. During those times, I've refused to focus on my outward circumstances. Instead, I've clung even tighter to what I deeply believe in my heart, which is that my future is bright and no one can prevent me from reaching my goals.

When I have found myself wondering if I'll ever ascend all those hills, I've thought of my grandfather who, long before the demise of apartheid, negotiated a major, groundbreaking deal with BMW. I've asked myself, "If he was able to find ways around all kinds of obstacles then, how much more should I be able to do so in these times?" I've also thought of what my mom tends to say to me when I'm dealing with injustice: "Lindi, that person means it for evil, but God is going to turn this around for your good." Armed with these thoughts and my faith, I've plowed ahead and continued to perform at the highest level possible, all the while building bridges with others, confident that sooner or later, there or somewhere else, I'd be coming out on top.

Or perhaps you find yourself struggling to land a job because your name "sounds Black" and some hiring managers may be reluctant to employ you, feeling that you won't fit the "mold" or "culture." Don't give up. Don't buy into the fear or lie that you'll never make it because you're Black. Keep moving. Climb that first hill, then the next, and the next, and the next.

When you get tempted to throw in the towel, think of the likes of Carl Brashear, whose story was memorialized in the movie *Men of Honor*. Mr. Brashear wrote more than a hundred letters, asking to be admitted to the Navy diving school, and once admitted, he had to overcome blatant racism, a deficient education, and an amputated leg in his quest to become the first Black US Navy diver. He made it and didn't allow anything or anyone to stand in his way. Keep on working—as he and many others like him have done—to find creative and constructive solutions to any obstacles you may be confronted with. Once you've made the right choices, exercise resilience! And along the way, see if you can't build bridges that connect you to others rather than tearing them down. This, I am sure, is the best way to move forward.

Although groups like Black Lives Matter would have us believe otherwise, the United States has made a great deal of progress in race relations since Jim Crow days. As a prime example, the idea of three Black Americans serving simultaneously as the president, attorney general, and secretary of the Department of Homeland Security of the United States was unthinkable not so long ago. More recently, *Black Panther*—a movie about a fictional nation in Africa, directed by a Black man (Ryan Coogler) and featuring an almost exclusively Black cast—smashed US box office records on its opening weekend, becoming the biggest superhero film ever. As a people, we are free to pursue our dreams. This speaks to how racially progressive we are as a whole. For the most part, we no longer have to deal with racism on a daily basis. Recent violent events in Charleston, South Carolina, and other cities around the United States remind us that there is still more progress to make, of course, but I don't believe that we should demonize an entire group or our country because of acts performed by extremists on the fringes of society. The best approach is to look forward in hope, be willing to do the hard work necessary to forge ahead, and partner with other race groups where possible to address any issues that still persist.

Tshoha, o Iketsetse![15]

One of my friends recently sent me a link to an online article about the advantages White South Africans have over the other race groups. I've seen articles like this before, which highlight the reasons why it is still so difficult for South African Blacks—a category that today in South Africa includes Indians and Coloureds—to get ahead or even to just catch up. These lists include items such as the following:

- *Social capital* – White people are more likely to come from educated families and to have family members and friends in high-level positions who can make introductions, get them into the "right places," and otherwise assist them.
- *Business knowledge* – White children are more likely to learn about business by listening to their parents talk around the dinner table and visiting their parents at work. White children learn how to shake hands, how to dress for and behave in high-level situations, and how to otherwise fit in to the business environment.
- *General knowledge* – White children learn more about the world from their parents than Black children do and are more likely to be familiar with history, literature, and so on. This gives them an advantage in the world of business, for they can bond with others by talking about various topics, such as Steve Jobs' legacy or the ski slopes.
- *Generational wealth* – Whites have always been able to purchase

property and have had access to better jobs and to loans, so they have been able to accumulate wealth and pass it on to the next generation.

- *Early childhood development* – White children are more likely to have access to good nutrition, health care, and education.
- *Being "one of us"* – White people automatically assume that other Whites are competent and well-behaved, while they hold different assumptions about "others."
- *Parents who can support themselves* – White people are much less likely to be forced to financially support their parents. This issue can be especially burdensome for younger Black people just starting off in their careers and beginning families of their own.

These are, for the most part, valid points. I say "for the most part" because these lists tend to generalize. Still, I suggest we use these recitations of woe, but only after converting them from reasons why we are still "victims" into action plans for success.

Does the Black community lack social capital? Do Black youngsters suffer from a lack of business knowledge? Then why aren't we spending more time developing and executing plans to address this on a large scale? How about inviting Black business people to be mentors and visit schools to engage with students? While we're at it, let's invite White, Asian, and every other "kind" of businessperson to meet with, learn about, encourage, and inspire Black youngsters. And how about encouraging more professional bodies to support students in their disciplines? In the United States, the National Association of Black Accountants mentors and offers scholarships to Black college students and new accountants, and offers professional development seminars to help Black accountants climb the ladder of success. A number of bodies in South Africa, including the Association for the Advancement of Black Accountants of Southern Africa and the Thuthuka Education Upliftment Fund, do the same. Can we encourage other organizations to do something similar? I am involved with the Big Brothers Big Sisters of Puget Sound, an organization that offers community and school-based mentoring as well as a workplace mentoring program for kids aged six to eighteen. Is there more that I as an individual can do? Can we motivate companies we work for— and even entire communities—to become involved in similar efforts?

Are many Black children not being properly fed or educated? Let's call upon our respective governments to provide the funding necessary to establish or give access to schools that provide a quality education for all children, and let's hold the governments accountable to that goal. If those leaders don't deliver, let's exercise our voting power and have them replaced with leaders who will. Let's stop being loyal to political parties that don't deliver on their promises and aren't accountable. Let's encourage businesses, social organizations, and community clubs to sponsor schools and students, and let's urge all parents (who are able) to help out at their children's schools. If funding schools and nutrition means cutting back on other items in the nation's budget, that's fine. Let's make preparing our children for the future our number one priority.

I don't have solutions to every issue on the list, and solutions will vary from country to country. But I do know that as long as we point to these lists—wherever in the world we might live—and say, "That's what's holding us back!" we will continue to focus on the past and lag behind. But if, instead, we make these action priority lists, we will begin building a dream for the future.

Can we go further than making these items action priorities? Can we make them points of pride or even acts of love? When I was doing my articles of internship in law fresh out of university, I bought a house for Mamkhulu outside of Soweto in what was then a predominately White middle-class neighborhood. It wasn't a mansion, just a two-bedroom, two-bathroom house with a loft and a lovely garden. Buying Mamkhulu a house meant that I couldn't buy one for myself, but I loved the idea that my grandmother—who gave so much to me—was now living in a house she could truly call her own. And it even had indoor plumbing with hot water, which meant that, for the first time in her life, she could take a bath in a full-sized bathtub in a bathroom of her own with "unlimited" hot water on tap! At the very same time, a White colleague of mine was buying a house for himself. His decision was financially sound, and I could have done the same in order to get an early start on building wealth. But faced with the choice of acting out of love or out of an interest in my bottom line, I chose love.

"Let Your Choices Reflect Your Hopes and Not Your Fears"

Once again, I acknowledge that apartheid in South Africa and slavery combined with Jim Crow in the United States have held us back. I also appreciate that as we are not yet living in a dispensation in which the races are fully reconciled, we may have to grapple with racism from time to time. But I am in favor of looking inward first, and then looking forward in hope and brotherhood.

I can almost hear the critics lining up to chastise me. Some may accuse me of putting all of the heavy lifting on Blacks and going too easy on Whites. They will say, "You're pretty smug, telling everyone to 'look to yourself,' but you went to private schools. You had a much better quality education than most Blacks!"

It's true that I went to private schools and had the benefit of picking up technical and soft skills I otherwise would not have had the opportunity to learn in a public Black school. But I had no money for books while attending private school, and after school, I returned home to Soweto, to the tiny house with the toilet outside and to dirt roads, poverty, crime, and all the rest. In fact, I was in some ways worse off, for unlike many other Black children, I was face-to-face with apartheid inequity every school day. I went in to the well-to-do White neighborhoods like Observatory; I saw the big houses with the giant green yards, and I studied with classmates who had money and opportunities I couldn't even imagine. I was surrounded by schoolmates whose moms or dads often dropped them off at school and picked them up afterward. I went to a birthday party in one of those amazing houses and saw a classmate receive more presents in one day than I would get in years! I ate pizza and hamburgers in their homes, foods that to them were commonplace but to me were so expensive that I could only afford to enjoy them as a treat at the end of each school quarter.

Then I went to Wits, and even though apartheid was crumbling, apartheid inequities were still shoved in my face as I struggled to find enough money to pay tuition—forget about things like buying books or new clothes. I had to go to the library every day to read the assigned material, and I was almost barred from returning to Wits in 1994 for failure to pay my fees. As I couldn't afford to buy any of the required study materials, it's really quite a miracle that I passed my classes and ultimately graduated with three degrees from Wits, and then went on to garner another from Boston University years later.

It would have been so easy for me to point the finger at others and say, "Why are they so much better off? Why is life so unfair?" Instead, I chose to focus on myself, to identify the things I had the power to work on and to improve. I chose to hold firmly to the things that made me stronger, including my faith and trust in God's power and ability. Guided by my parents and grandparents, I learned early on that there are two approaches in life. Either you focus on yourself and the things you can do to improve your life, or you focus on "them," on inequities and inequalities, on what they have versus what you do not have. Either you focus on hope and possibilities—no matter how slight—or on bitterness and anger.

We can spend our time blaming and being angry at Whites. We can make ludicrous demands of them, along the lines of those issued by the cofounder of Black Lives Matter Louisville in response to the events in Charlottesville in 2017.[16] That is certainly an option. But I don't believe this approach will move us forward. We can't race toward our goals if we're mentally and emotionally bound to the weight of the past; we cannot be free if the past still has a hold on us. We must find a way to forgive, and in so doing, to let go of the past. As we do, it is important for us to remember that each person must be judged as an individual, that not every White person is racist, and that even those who struggle with racism have the capacity to change. It is also important to keep in mind that forgiveness is not earned but given and that it is not always a one-off act. Sometimes, especially when wounds run deep, one needs to return to the well of forgiveness and draw from its depths, day after day, until the bitterness in one's heart has been washed away. Ideally, we would do so because we empathize with our wrongdoers' humanity and appreciate the fact that we, too, have vices and that we are also on a journey of learning how to overcome these. If not for that reason, we should do so because it's good for our mental and emotional well-being. Because doing so will allow us to move forward unencumbered. There's power in that. That's not to say we shouldn't challenge racism where it manifests itself—far from it. But I believe that the more "whole" we are, the more we'll be able to discern whether we are dealing with a matter of true injustice or not, and where we are, to be powerful and effective when addressing it.

In some cases, we're absolutely right; injustice truly is in play, and we should work to address it as constructively as possible. In other instances, the injustice is only a perception triggered more by our wounds than by reality, and it does not exist; in other cases, it does exist but we also have unclean hands and must accept our part in it, even while calling out the wrong on the other side.

When we claim discrimination in instances where there is none, or where we may be at fault also, we make it more difficult for our cause to be taken seriously when injustice is, in fact, occurring. In the 1950s, Dr. Martin Luther King Jr. chose a strategy that involved a "collection of facts to determine whether injustices are alive." He wanted to make sure that discrimination was truly in play before acting, even though back then, racism and discrimination were common here and, in general, legally sanctioned. The probability of discrimination was incredibly high, but even so, Dr. King wanted to be sure. Today, with laws that discriminated against Blacks having been overturned, don't we have a greater obligation to think twice before making any claims that racism is the cause of our inability to put our lives and those of our children on an upward trajectory, and a greater obligation to look into any anger or bitterness we may harbor against others?

For me, there was never really a choice between focusing on bitterness or on possibilities, because going back at least three generations, my family's path has been fixed on the future. Yes, life was unfair, and my father paid the ultimate price for that unfairness. But he, like millions of others, fought to right the wrongs, and when the walls of apartheid came crumbling down, I was prepared to move into the brand-new future.

Thanks to the generations before me who believed in the future, who chose *ubuntu* over bitterness and faith over hopelessness, I learned that the path forward always begins with a look inward. This gave me the determination to improve myself in every way possible and to embrace all others who are willing to be embraced as friends. That is the gift my forebears gave me, and that is the gift I wish to pass on to my children and to all those I come in contact with, if they are willing to receive it.

When we reflexively blame others for *all* of our problems, we declare to the world—and even worse, to ourselves—that we are perpetual victims in perpetual need of extra help and support. Wouldn't it be more empowering to see ourselves as a people who have come through severe trials and are just beginning to tap into our amazing potential? We've come this far despite all the crap we've had to deal with. Think how much further we can go, now that we've overcome apartheid, Jim Crow, and so many other instances of bias and discrimination. Whether in South Africa, in the United States, or in any number of other countries, we are living in a dispensation our forebears could only dream of, and we have opportunities they could not even imagine. Rather than point our fingers at the past or at others, let's point and look to the sky and make that our goal.

Rather than constantly saying "We need more," let's continually remind ourselves that we have the ability to do so much more. And by the way, in the past, collectively, we *have* done so much more. In the early years of the twentieth century, Black Americans in Tulsa, Oklahoma, built a thriving community in a section centered around Greenwood Avenue. Despite restrictive race laws, the Greenwood Black community prospered. They became doctors and attorneys and opened real estate offices and other businesses. They published two newspapers of their own and supported more than a dozen churches. There were banks, cafés, movie theaters, and hotels, all created by and catering to the Black community. There was even a school system that provided an excellent education to Black children. So prosperous was Greenwood that it was known as "the Black Wall Street."

It was all destroyed in race riots in 1921, and there is no excuse for this reprehensible act of violent racism. Still, Greenwood and similar communities prove that even under restrictive and degrading circumstances, Blacks can be as prosperous, creative, community-oriented, and forward-looking as anyone else. I don't know what it would take to create something similar today, for conditions have changed greatly. I don't even know if we would want to recreate a "closed" Black community, as Greenwood was. But I do know that we Blacks are as intelligent, talented, creative, devoted, determined, and loving as anyone else. I do know that there is *no* reason that we, as a collective, cannot succeed—and marvelously so!—once we decide that we *will* overcome, no matter how difficult the path forward may be.

About a year ago, I attended a work conference on race and ethnicity. An audience member who was Black asked one of the presenters, who was also Black, "How can I have hope that I will progress in an organization where, from the top down, no one looks like me?" She was speaking to the fact that even though Blacks comprise about twenty-two percent of the total workforce, only six percent of management is Black.[17]

The presenter gave a lengthy response that, in effect, boiled down to this: "You don't need anyone to look to. We believed in ourselves long before anyone else did."

What a powerful message! And what a powerful reminder as well, for when we were oppressed under apartheid or colonialism in Africa, or held as slaves or ground down by Jim Crow here in the US, we believed in ourselves. We believed in our humanity and value long before others joined us in our fight for freedom and equality. We believed that we could overcome, and—equally important—we believed that we had the power, directly or through our faith, to make it happen.

Let's channel that spirit of power and faith again!

WHAT GIVES YOU HOPE AND COURAGE?

I thought I was finished writing this book, but as an author-friend once said, "There's always one more issue to consider lurking about."

In my case, the final thought came as my mother Esther was reading the final draft of the final chapter. She suddenly remembered two incidents she'd gone through that had been buried in her memory for decades. In her words:

> I remember one night when my father was away, so only my mother and I were home. I was maybe twelve years old. Late at night, when all was dark and we were in bed, sleeping, the house was suddenly surrounded by men banging on the doors and windows. Over the banging there were frightening shouts:
>
> "Police! Police!"
>
> "Where's John Langa?"
>
> "John Langa, John Langa!" The police were pounding so brutally that they could have brought the door down! Then the policemen—all of them were White and all armed—went through the house, looking everywhere, shouting over and over, "Where is John Langa!?" This went

on until they were satisfied that he was not in the house, and they left. My mother and I were traumatized, and we spent the rest of the night trying to recuperate.

This happened a few times.

And it wasn't only the authorities we had to fear. When I was about fourteen years old, we lived in Orlando East and my cousins were living in Jabulane. One day, I took the bus to visit my cousins; this was a half-an-hour-long trip. When you got off the bus, you still had a good fifteen minutes to travel by foot. I was walking, not thinking anything could happen to me. Suddenly these young men came, four or five of them, and they rushed for me.

"Hey you, come here!" they called. I looked at them, and I started running. They ran after me—they wanted to rape me. To this day, I don't know how I outran so many boys. When I arrived at my cousin's place, I was terrified. It was such a frightening and demeaning experience for me.

Living in a world where it was normal for young men to run after and rape women, and where the police could harass or arrest you for no reason at all, was terribly frightening. It wasn't just the moments or minutes of actual confrontation; the fear was everywhere. It was in the air we breathed. We were all vulnerable, in so many ways.

Like Mom, I grew up in an environment suffused with fear—fear of the authorities, fear of racists, fear of being branded an *impimpi*,[18] and fear of the violence within the community—and, for women especially, fear of sexual abuse. Statistics vary, but it is generally agreed that about one-third of South African women were raped back then and that only a small percentage of these rapes were reported to the authorities. My experiences were similar in kind to my mom's, although, thankfully, to a slightly lesser degree. I did have my encounter with the jackrollers, and I learned early in life to tread carefully around the *tsotsis*. I saw plenty of Casspirs—military-style vehicles—stationed at various points in the townships during states of emergency to intimidate us and suppress anti-apartheid activity.

The police in the Casspirs never bothered or even approached me, but you always knew they were there, and what they represented during those times.

As my mother and I talked about the fears we experienced, I began to wonder how much fear stops us. To what extent is fear a mental roadblock that prevents us from even imagining a better future?

In this book, I've frequently spoken about choice, and I firmly believe that no matter what our circumstances, we must cling fiercely to our ability to make choices. The choices available to us may be few and may seem feeble, but it is only by making the right choices that we can rise above our circumstances. And with support and guidance, it is possible to make right choices even when fear is "in the air." Although Mom and I suffered through many fearful experiences, we had safe havens and were embraced and guided by loving people. At Sacred Heart, for example, I was taught by my teachers—including many White ones—that I was as good as anyone else, and that I had untapped potential. In church, I was reminded that God loves me as much as He loves everyone else and that He has great plans for me; at home, I was lovingly guided by my mother, Mamkhulu, John Langa, and my great-grandmother Gertrude. When I reconnected with my father, he did the same. This gave me a sense of hope and the courage to make the right choices.

But what happens if you lack safe havens and supportive guides? I recently watched a video about life in certain sections of the city of Baltimore, where crime is the norm and violence is so frequent that much of it goes unremarked upon. It only takes a few statistics to make one shudder:

- According to the US Drug Enforcement Agency, Baltimore "has the highest per capita heroin addiction rate in the country."[19]
- The 2017 homicide rate in Baltimore was 55.8 per 100,000 people, which earns Baltimore the dubious honor of being the deadliest big city in the nation. (The second-place city, New Orleans, suffered 40.0 homicides per 100,000 population.)[20]

- Most of the homicides in Baltimore are related to drugs and gang activity.[21]
- Blacks are far and away the most likely to be killed, with 90% of the homicide victims in the city being Black.
- Black residents of Baltimore earn, on average, only 55% of what White residents earn.[22]
- In 2013, the unemployment rate for young Black men was 37%, compared to 10% for young White men.[23]
- The poverty rate for Blacks in Baltimore is 27.5%, significantly higher than that of Whites (12.8%) and Asians (18.9%).[24]
- Poverty is linked to health and longevity, with the residents of Upton and Druid Heights (median annual income of $13,388) living an average of 63 years, while residents of nearby Roland Park (median annual income of $90,492) are likely to live until the age of 83.[25]
- In 2010, out of every 100,000 Blacks in Baltimore, an average of 1,437 were incarcerated, as compared to 311 Hispanics and 310 Whites. For the state of Maryland overall, Blacks make up 29% of the population and 68% of the prison population, while Whites comprise 55% of the population and only 27% of the prison population.[26]

When you put these statistics together with the many others that describe the unpleasant truth about life in certain areas of Baltimore, you realize that many youngsters are being raised in an environment dripping with fear, that they are surrounded by violence and failure, and that there is a definite lack of safe havens and supportive guides. In far too many cases, children are being raised by only one parent, and that woman—for it is generally a mother rather than a father—may be weighed down with too many responsibilities to allow her to adequately fulfill her parental duties, or she may have substance-abuse issues. Many of these children attend public schools where teachers have their hands full just trying to keep order—or in some cases, the children have just stopped attending school. There are few safe havens for these children, for they are as likely to be exposed to drugs at home as they are on the street, and gang activity can make going to the park or to a friend's house a risky endeavor. Family and community relationships have been shattered, and government resources have been stretched to the limits.

I'm not saying that every child in the afflicted areas of Baltimore lives like this, but there are enough to make me wonder if it's always possible for someone to make the right choices. If, as in one case I've read about, the mother is an addict and the child first meets Dad at the age of fifteen—and only because the child is entering jail as the father is completing his sentence—do they even know what those choices may be? Is it at all realistic for me to tell such children that they must pull themselves up by their own bootstraps?

What about children who are regularly exposed to violence, to shootings, beatings, robberies, and more? What happens to kids who are victims, or who witness these horrible events, or who are regularly woken up by the sounds of police sirens, or who pass memorials to victims of violence every day on the street as they walk to school or play? The *Baltimore Sun* has reported that:

> Studies have piled up showing that in the tangle of tough, intractable issues like poverty and drug addiction, exposure to violence is a major factor damaging children's health. The stress that fills their little bodies breeds anxiety and depression, making it hard for them to concentrate in school. In fact, research has found that such experiences hurt the development of crucial areas of their brains — those involving attention, memory and behavior control. In the worst cases, children walk around with symptoms of post-traumatic stress disorder no different from those plaguing soldiers who have fought on the front lines.[27]

Certainly not all children exposed to the toxic stew of violence, poverty, and drugs develop symptoms of PTSD, but many do. And many others undoubtedly suffer in ways that stunt their emotional and intellectual growth yet do not rise to the level where they are noticed. Can we expect children in such an environment to make the right choices and thrive?

Some do, and succeed beyond all expectations. For example, in 2017, Isaiah Cooper became the youngest Black American pilot to fly all the way across the United States. Age seventeen when he flew into the record books, Isaiah was reared in Compton, California, a city that has long been known for poverty, unemployment, drugs, gangs, and drive-by shootings.

But lacking guidance and support, other youngsters struggle. Because they lack, we must give. Change that encompasses the elimination of violence, and adoption of measures I outlined in the last chapter—such as the prioritization of education, exercise in self-discipline, a shift back to the maintenance of two-parent families (or the provision of access to both parents), and so forth—is certainly needed in Baltimore and other Black communities like Baltimore. In the meantime, children are falling through the cracks. We must put an end to that!

One of the most important things we can give children in this position is early intervention to help them cope with the horrors to which they are exposed. This aid can take many forms, including dedicating funds so teachers may be trained to recognize and deal with the signs of distress in youngsters, even those as young as two or three. Rather than trying to discipline them when they act out or shut themselves in, teachers can be trained to help them express and release their often-suppressed feelings, and to guide them through the very difficult process of learning, or relearning, how to value themselves and to see for themselves a better future. Perhaps time could be allocated every day to allow children to think about their futures, about the different ways in which their lives might play out, and about all the possibilities ahead. The teachers themselves can become safe havens who help instill hope and courage in their hearts, rather than just another prod to anger or resentment.

Another powerful form of aid is when former members of the community—who have been through the worst—come back to help others avoid failure. One such person is Tyree Colion, a Baltimore rapper who went to jail at the age of fifteen, serving ten years for second-degree murder. He went back to prison after release, this time for violating parole. Since his second release in 2012, he has worked to reduce violence in the community. Today, he is known for the "No-Shoot Zones" he creates in Baltimore and in other cities by spray-painting that message on the walls of buildings where people have been shot down. He speaks with the voice of experience, and his experience shouts out that it is possible to rise above miserable circumstances, even if you have fallen and have been discarded by others.

Knowing what Tyree Colion is doing, I must ask myself: What am I doing to help provide support and guidance to children who find themselves in such circumstances, and to other youngsters as well? Sure, I have the honor of being a young lady's mentor through Big Brothers Big Sisters of Puget Sound, but am I doing enough? Are we all doing enough?

What Is Your Fear?

Fortunately, the majority of us do not live lives in which making good choices is such a difficult proposition. Yet we often struggle with making good choices, as individuals and as communities.

What issues are you having difficulty with, and what fear is holding you back and preventing you from making the choices required to move your life forward? Fear of not fitting in? Fear of failure? Is there some way for you to surround yourself with people who will help you believe that success is within reach so that you can be hopeful about the future and you can have courage to make good choices?

And what stands in the way of our reaching out to others so that we might help them make the positive choices they need to make?

I believe that every positive choice—no matter who makes it, where, when, or why—rebounds to the benefit of us all. Each time we make a positive choice, and each time we help others do the same, we make the world a better place for us all—a world in which, in the spirit of *ubuntu*, we affirm our connection to and our interdependence on each other.

NOTES

1   In South Africa today, the term "Black" mostly refers to those who had been classified under apartheid as "Black," "Coloured," and "Indian." Back then, this term did not include Indians and Coloureds.

2   I use the term "Coloured" throughout the book as a reference to a racial category that was established under apartheid.

3   See Chapter Five for more on *ubuntu*.

4   "Tsotsis" is a South African slang word referring to a gang member or urban Black criminal.

5   A Bantustan was a Black homeland, a so-called "independent nation," carved out of South African territory and given over to a particular tribe or tribal group. Although nominally independent, the Bantustans were entirely dependent on and subject to the will of the South African government. Establishing Bantustans was the White government's way of arguing that Blacks are not oppressed; rather, they have their own "freedoms" that must be exercised in their own "independent" countries. But the Bantustans were never economically viable and simply became reservoirs of cheap Black labor for the White urbanized, industrialized, and prosperous South Africa.

6   The primary exception was a Coloured man who drove my visually impaired grandfather, and his sister, who sometimes spent a fair amount of time at my grandparents' house.

7   The infamous "pencil test" was one of several used to distinguish Whites from "others" during apartheid. These tests were felt to be necessary because it was not always obvious whether one was White or Coloured

(meaning mixed race). So if there was doubt, the person might have to undergo the pencil test. A pencil was pushed into the hair on the individual's head; if the pencil fell to the floor, the person was judged to be White. But if the hair was kinky or curly enough to hold on to the pencil, the person was classified as Coloured.

8 Information taken from Table 5: Enrollment in South African Universities 1994 in "Apartheid and the Universities" by The Ratcatcher, *Politicsweb*, January 17, 2012. Accessible at http://www.politicsweb.co.za/news-and-analysis/apartheid-and-the-universities. Viewed May 16, 2017.

9 SASO stands for South African Student Organization, which was the predecessor of SASCO. SRC stands for the Student Representative Council.

10 "Report for December 1993 & January 1994," Independent Board of Inquiry, Johannesburg, South Africa: 22.

11 I identify as a Black American. I understand, however, that others may disagree with my view, feeling that because I was not raised in the United States, I cannot understand what it means to be a Black American from a cultural perspective.

12 A CNBC article reports that "According to the St. Louis Fed's study, Asian-American median wealth in 2013 stood at $91,440, about 70 percent of the level of whites. Their wealth increased 43 percent since 1989 (inflation adjusted), Emmons and his co-authors at the Fed found. Whites gained only 3 percent to $134,008 in that same time period." See Hailey Lee, "How Asian-Americans are transforming the face of US wealth," *CNBC*, March 15, 2015. Accessible at https://www.cnbc.com/2015/03/15/americans-are-transforming-the-face-of-us-wealth.html. Viewed September 1, 2018.

13 Lauren Camera, "African-American Students Lagging Far Behind," *US News*, December 11, 2015. Accessible at https://www.usnews.com/news/articles/2015/12/11/african-american-students-lagging-far-behind. Viewed September 28, 2017.

14 Sonali Kohi, "If Asian Americans Saw White Americans the Way White Americans See Black Americans," *Quartz*, April 30, 2015. Accessible at https://qz.com/395207/if-asian-americans-saw-white-americans-the-way-white-americans-see-black-americans/. Viewed January 24, 2018.

15 This is a Sesotho term meaning "Wake up, and do it yourself."

16 Chanelle Helm, "White people, here are 10 requests from a Black Lives Matter leader," *LEO Weekly*, August 16, 2017. Accessible at https://www.leoweekly.com/2017/08/white-people/. Viewed September 25, 2018.

17 "Diversity at Amazon." Accessible at https://www.amazon.com/b/ref=tb_surl_diversity/?node=10080092011. Viewed February 20, 2018.

18 An *impimpi* is a Zulu word for an informer.

19 Carter M. Yang, "Part I: Baltimore Is the U.S. Heroin Capital," *ABC News*, March 14, 2018. Accessible at https://abcnews.go.com/US/story?id=92699&page=1. Viewed September 17, 2018.

20 Aamer Madhani, "Baltimore is the nation's most dangerous city," *USA Today*, February 19, 2018. Accessible at https://www.usatoday.com/story/news/2018/02/19/homicides-toll-big-u-s-cities-2017/302763002/. Viewed September 17, 2018.

21 Gary Gately, "Baltimore is more murderous than Chicago. Can anyone save the city from itself?" *The Guardian*, November 2, 2017. Accessible at https://www.theguardian.com/us-news/2017/nov/02/baltimore-murder-rate-homicides-ceasefire. Viewed September 17, 2018.

22 Jordan Malter, "Baltimore's economy in black and white," *CNN Money*, April 29, 2015. Accessible at https://money.cnn.com/2015/04/29/news/economy/baltimore-economy/index.html. Viewed September 17, 2018.

23 Malter, "Baltimore's economy in black and white."

24 "Baltimore, Maryland Population 2018," *World Population Review*. Accessible at http://worldpopulationreview.com/us-cities/baltimore-population/. Viewed September 17, 2018.

25 Malter, "Baltimore's economy in black and white."

26 "Maryland Profile," Prison Policy Initiative. Accessible at https://www.prisonpolicy.org/profiles/MD.html. Viewed September 17, 2018.

27 Andrea K. McDaniels, "Collateral Damage: Advocates aim to save Baltimore children from impact of violence," Baltimore Sun, December 14, 2014. Accessible at http://www.baltimoresun.com/health/bs-md-health-violence-121114-story.html. Viewed September 17, 2018.

CPSIA information can be obtained
at www.ICGtesting.com
Printed in the USA
LVHW081110140619
621233LV00010B/29/P